D1459282

H46 066 994 9

AMAZING & EXTRAORDINARY FACTS

TRAINS
& RAILWAYS

AMAZING & EXTRAORDINARY FACTS

TRAINS & RAILWAYS

JULIAN HOLLAND

David and Charles

A DAVID & CHARLES BOOK
© F&W Media International Ltd 2011

David & Charles is an imprint of F&W Media International, Ltd
Brunel House, Forde Close, Newton Abbot, TQ12 4PU, UK

F&W Media International, Ltd is a subsidiary of F+W Media, Inc.,
4700 East Galbraith Road
Cincinnati OH45236, USA

A catalogue record for this book is available from the British Library.

ISBN-13: 978-0-7153-3911-4
ISBN-10: 0-7153-3911-7

Printed in Finland by Bookwell
for David & Charles
Brunel House, Newton Abbot, Devon

10 9 8 7 6 5 4 3 2 1

Commissioning Editor: Neil Baber
Assistant Editor: Felicity Barr
Senior Designer: Victoria Marks
Senior Production Controller: Kelly Smith

F+W Media publish high quality books on a wide range of subjects.
For more great book ideas visit:
www.rubooks.co.uk

CONTENTS

Introduction	6	Push Me – Pull You/1	80
Happy Christmas!	10	Named Trains	82
Keeping an Eye on Costs	13	Glow in the Dark	84
A Bridge too Far	14	Who was that Man?	87
Steam Dreams	18	A–Z of London's Main Railway Stations	92
Stop Press	21		
Tickets Please!	23	The Old, Slow & Dirty Lives On	98
Chip Vans	26	Wartime Facts and Figures	100
The Tiddley Dyke	28	Southern Railway Famous Trains	104
New for Old	32	Stop Press	107
Ghost Trains	37	Made in Scotland	108
Doing it Legally	40	Railway Journeys Trivia	111
Evenin' All!	42	Railways That Never Were	114
Order! Order!	46	Railway Museums	116
Brush Strokes	48	Push Me – Pull You/2	122
The First Severn Bridge	51	A Kent Railway Village	124
Small is Beautiful	54	Glasgow Termini	126
The Slow, Miserable & Jolty	56	Goodbye Hazel, Doris, Audrey, Vera, Gwen and Mona	130
Stop Press	59		
War Service	60	The Clockwork Orange	132
GWR Famous Trains	63	A Railway Coalition	134
Reservoir Dogs	66	Chinese Laundries	136
Tram Lines	70	A Railway-Owned Electrical Tramway	138
Happy Birthday, GWR	72		
Stop Press	77	Index	140
Steam Locomotive Nicknames	78	Picture Credits	144

INTRODUCTION

This book, the third in my series of *Amazing & Extraordinary Railways Facts*, is filled with even more stories and obscure facts and figures that I know all railway lovers enjoy. Of course, as many of my readers now know, it all started for me in my home town of Gloucester back in the 1950s when I, along with most of my school chums, would spend our weekends and school holidays watching (and noting) the seemingly endless procession of steam trains that converged on our city.

Now sadly demolished, Gloucester Eastgate station always had a special place in my heart – only a five-minute walk from my childhood home and my regular stamping ground during my trainspotting days in the late 1950s and early 1960s. It was also the station where we embarked on our annual summer holiday – my father didn't own a car and we always headed south on a convoluted train journey to our destination. Whether it be Exmouth, Lyme Regis, Woolacombe or Perranporth the journey there and back was always the highlight of the holiday for me.

I first discovered the delights of the station when I was around 11 years old by which age I had caught the trainspotting bug badly and, armed with

notebook and pencil, would spend most Saturdays at the north end of the curving island platform of this former Midland Railway station watching the comings and goings of trains on the Bristol to Birmingham main line. It was also a good vantage point to watch activity at Horton Road shed and trains on the ex-GWR line out of Central station. There was never a dull moment!

Summer Saturdays were pure bliss at Eastgate, despite missing some holiday expresses which ran via the Gloucester avoiding line; there was a never-ending procession of trains: ex-LMS 'Black 5' and 'Jubilee' Class 4-6-0s on trains between the North and South such as the 'Devonian' and 'Pines Express' with Bristol Barrow Road 'Patriot' Class 5 4-6-0s (No. 45506 'The Royal Pioneer Corps' and No. 45519 'Lady Godiva' were regular performers) and Gloucester Barnwood's ancient 2P 4-4-0s or BR Standard Class 5 4-6-0s on local stopping trains to Bristol or Birmingham. In 1960 Barrow Road had a total of nine 'Jubilees' and regulars such as No. 45651 'Shovell', No. 45662 'Kempenfelt', No. 45682 'Trafalgar' and No. 45699 'Galatea' were seen on an almost daily basis heading Bristol to Newcastle expresses and the evening TPO. Despite all of this mainly ex-LMS scene the one daily intruder (but most welcome) was the 'Cornishman' from Wolverhampton Low Level to Penzance which was always headed by an immaculate Stafford Road 'Castle' such as No. 5045 'Earl of Dudley' or No. 5088 'Llanthony Abbey' hauling a rake of smart Mk 1 brown and cream coaches – on a summer Saturday this train ran in two portions with the second part heading for Paignton.

To add to this glorious scene the comings and goings from Horton Road shed and in and out of Central station could also be witnessed from the north end of Eastgate's island platform - trains to and from Paddington arriving or departing behind one of 85B's well-groomed

'Castle' 4-6-0s such as No. 5017 'The Gloucestershire Regiment 28th, 61st', No. 5071 'Spitfire' or No. 7000 'Viscount Portal' while Class '5101' 2-6-2Ts or even occasionally '9400' 0-6-0PTs struggled manfully with the eight-coach trains to and from Cheltenham St James.

Now, as a small lad growing up in Gloucester I wasn't really aware of a major conflict going on nearly halfway round the world. Back in the early 1950s when I was knee high to a grasshopper our local boys in the Gloucestershire Regiment were part of the United Nations (mainly US) forces that were grappling with the Communist Chinese-backed North Korean invasion of South Korea. The savage fighting swung back and forth up the Asian peninsula until there was a stalemate, followed by protracted peace talks and an armistice which was signed on 27 July 1953.

However, one action in this god-forsaken country has since passed into legend and was soon to be recognised by the management of the Western Region of British Railways. In April 1951 the A, B, C and D Companies of the 1st Battalion, Gloucestershire Regiment, along with the Royal Northumberland Fusiliers, the Royal Ulster Rifles and a Belgian battalion, were strategically positioned on hilltops overlooking the Imjin River, north of Seoul – their task was to hold back the massed hordes of Chinese soldiers who were threatening to take the South Korean capital for the second time in a year.

Led by their Commanding Officer, Colonel Fred Carne, the Glosters held out on their hilltop (appropriately named Gloucester Hill) against waves of thousands of Chinese soldiers, inflicting enormous casualties on them. Finally surrounded by the enemy, withdrawal was well-nigh impossible for the Glosters so they courageously fought on until their ammunition ran out. In their hundreds the survivors were finally rounded up by the Chinese and sent off to spend more than two years in appalling prisoner-of-war camps in the North. The Glosters' heroic stand on Gloucester Hill has since gone down in history.

Eventually released from their prison camps in North Korea, the survivors of the Gloucestershire Regiment – including Colonel Carne who had spent most of the time in solitary confinement – arrived back home to a rapturous welcome from the people of Gloucester. As a young lad I can well remember watching the 'Glorious Glosters' marching through the streets of the city, the indomitable Colonel Carne at their head, for a service of thanksgiving in the cathedral. The regimental colours along with a wooden cross carved by Colonel Carne while in prison camp can still be seen in the cathedral today.

Rewind to July 1932 when the GWR's latest 'Castle' Class 4-6-0 No. 5017 'St Donat's Castle' emerged sparkling new from Swindon Works. The loco spent the next 22 years working express trains out of Paddington until the Western Region of British Railways decided to honour the heroic Glosters' stand at the Imjin River by renaming the locomotive. Fitted with one of the largest brass nameplates on any ex-GWR loco, No. 5017 was renamed 'The Gloucestershire Regiment 28th, 61st' at a ceremony in April 1954 and appropriately spent the rest of its working life allocated to Horton Road depot in Gloucester.

I have many happy memories of this locomotive which I saw on a regular basis on the way to and from school each day, often working the 8.19am 'Cheltenham Spa Express' from Gloucester Central to Paddington and return. Displaced by 'Warship' diesel hydraulics, No. 5017 was finally withdrawn in September 1962 after covering nearly 600,000 miles in its lifetime and was ingloriously cutup at Cashmore's scrap yard in Newport. One of the two enormous brass nameplates along with the Sphinx badge and a cabside numberplate can be seen in the Soldiers of Gloucestershire Museum in the old Custom House in Gloucester Docks. I wish I owned the other one!

HAPPY CHRISTMAS!
The story of a railway Christmas in 1903

Christmas was once the busiest period of the year for the railways and the extra passenger and parcels traffic generated placed an enormous burden on the system. At the beginning of the 20th century paid holidays didn't exist and most people worked up to Christmas Eve, taking only two days off before returning to their city toils. To cope with this mass exodus special trains were run at midnight on Christmas Eve from London termini to principal stations, carrying to their country homes thousands of worn-out workers – if the part that our railways played at Christmas had been properly understood then there would have been a collection for the Railway Benevolent Institution at every Christmas dinner table.

Figures released by the London & South Western Railway at the end of 1903 show just how busy this period was for them. On the four days preceding Christmas nearly 100,000 tickets were issued at Waterloo station – these excluded previously bought season tickets or tickets that had been bought at the company's city offices. In the course of an ordinary day there were about 1,000 trains working in and out of Waterloo but on 23 and 24 December the magnitude of bookings necessitated the running of most main line trains in duplicate, adding about 50 more trains to the daily total.

The majority of the post and parcels sent around the country in the days preceding Christmas was also carried by the railways. This was a massive undertaking with railway porters employed to load and unload vast quantities of mail and parcels on and off trains – during the seven days prior to Christmas, 1903, the London & North Western Railway handled 35,000 food hampers at Euston alone and to facilitate this work a special large shed, 2340ft long and 40ft wide, was erected in Maiden Lane. The company ran six special trains to and from Euston on these days just to carry parcels and hampers while at the Midland Railway's terminus of St Pancras around 100,000 parcels were handled. Special milk, fruit, meat and fish trains were also run from the provinces into

London – the LSWR had to run four extra trains just for the conveyance of milk churns on each of the four days before Christmas, while the meat specials carrying 'prime Scotch' from north of the border were considered even more important than the 'Flying Scotsman'! With the Smithfield Show also taking place the LNWR's Broad Street and Camden goods stations handled 2,214 tons of meat in the week ending 23 December.

The special working notice book issued by the GWR to its staff for Christmas, 1903 makes interesting reading. Special trains laid on included the 'Marlborough College Special', the 'Cheltenham Lady Collegians', and trains to carry boys home from Clifton College, Malvern College and Cheltenham College. 'Special Parcels Trains' were also run that had precedence over goods trains. Special vans were attached to the New Milford to Paddington parcels train to carry Irish poultry traffic. Altogether there were no less than 90 pages in the GWR's special Christmas notice, all referring to extra trains laid on between 18 and 25 December.

Needless to say, despite railway staff's hard work, there were some parcels that failed to reach their destination, usually because of incomplete or incorrect addresses. As some of these parcels contained perishable goods they were sold for what they could fetch. Items from the 'salvaged' parcels list included a barrel of oysters, a brace of pheasants, a hare, a turkey in feathers, a goose, four rabbits, goose dressed, box containing cake, puddings and photo and a box containing pork pies, sausages and pork.. A few people obviously had their Christmas festivities spoilt by the non-arrival of these goodies. Non-perishable items that also failed to get delivered for the same reason ranged from a tin tray from a parrot's cage and a parcel of trouser linings to two motor tyres.

Severe frost and fog at this time of the year also brought its problems – out of 313 down passenger trains arriving at Crewe during the four days before Christmas, 1903, 80 were half an hour late, 83 were from one to two hours late, and 15 were over two hours behind time. Up passenger trains fared just as badly and goods trains were shunted out of the way into sidings to wait until the pressure was over.

KEEPING AN EYE ON COSTS
A practical economy campaign for railways

Cut-backs and economies during times of recession aren't new. In connection with an economy campaign that was carried out by a certain railway company in the late 1920s some interesting statistics were prepared by the General Manager and included in a circular issued to all members of his staff. Many of the comparisons instituted were certainly striking and they couldn't fail to impress upon all who read the circular that economy was worthwhile even in the smallest and cheapest articles. Here are a few representative items from the list:

One lead pencil equals the haulage of one bag of maize for ten miles

One penholder equals the haulage of one bag of fertilizer (200lb) for five miles

One packet of mixed pins equals the haulage of one bag of fertilizer (100lb) for 10 miles

One large blotting pad equals the haulage of one ton of sand for 100 miles

One small blotting pad equals the haulage of one ton of crushed stone for 27 miles

One scribbling pad equals the haulage of one bag of lime (200lb) for 18 miles

One shorthand notebook equals the haulage of one bag of cement (187lb) for 13 miles

One truck buffer equals the haulage of ten tons of coal for 89 miles

One coupling link equals the haulage of one ton of fertilizer for 65 miles

One coupling pin equals the haulage of one ton of bones for 87 miles

One coach screw equals the haulage of one bag of coal (200lb) for 13 miles

One fishplate equals the haulage of one ton of salt for 16 miles

A BRIDGE TOO FAR
The story of the long forgotten Solway Viaduct

By the mid-19th century the manufacturing prosperity of the rich mining district of north Lanarkshire in Scotland depended entirely on the output from around 50 local coal and ironstone mines. These provided fuel and raw materials for the numerous steel furnaces, brass and iron foundries, engineering shops, oil and fireclay works and a host of other industries found around the industrial town of Airdrie. But before long the ironstone mines were becoming depleted of their best ores and the owners of the Calderbank Steel & Coal Company were forced to look further afield for supplies of this raw material.

A hundred miles south of Airdrie the haematite iron ore mines of West Cumbria were experiencing boom times and, by the early 1860s, much of their output was being carried by rail to north Lanarkshire. The journey via Carlisle and the Caledonian Railway's main line northwards was lengthy and costly and soon proposals were being put forward by several Cumbrian and Dumfries businessmen to build a new and shorter line bypassing Carlisle. And so the Solway Junction Railway was born.

Authorised in 1864, the 20½-mile line between Brayton, on the Maryport & Carlisle Railway, and Kirtlebridge, on the Caledonian main line north of Gretna, also involved the building of what was then the longest railway viaduct in the world. Although extending to a total length of 2,544yds, including embankments, from shore to shore the actual length of the bridge over the shifting sands of the Solway Firth was 1,940yds. It was a major undertaking for the time and took 3½ years to build; its 193 wrought-iron spans supported on cast-iron piles weighed a total of nearly 2,900 tons. The piles, supposedly protected from the tide and sands by timber cladding, were driven in at low tide from a fleet of five barges, but some gloom and doom merchants predicted that the viaduct was a white elephant and would soon be torn apart by the tides and shifting sands. South of Whitrigg the new railway obtained running powers over the North British Railway's Silloth branch as far as Abbey Town. From

here a new line was built to Brayton where it connected with the Maryport &
Carlisle Railway.

Worked from the outset by the Caledonian Railway, the new line opened
for freight in 1869 and for passengers in 1870. The pessimistic predictions
about the viaduct soon became a reality with ice causing many problems. The
cost of maintenance was high but so, too, were the revenues earned by the
railway. The Caledonian Railway took over the Solway Junction Railway in
1895 but its usefulness by then was drawing to a close – cheaper imported iron
ore gradually taking the place of dwindling West Cumbrian ore. Apart from
what became a branch line from Kirtlebridge to Annan, the rest of the railway
including the viaduct was temporarily closed for the duration of World
War I. Despite reopening in 1920 the viaduct by now was in poor shape and
the much reduced traffic using it hardly warranted the cost of repairs.

The end came on 20 May 1921 when all services south of Annan over the
viaduct ceased, although the 5½-mile branch line from Kirtlebridge to Annan
continued to operate until 1931 when it, too, closed. The Caledonian Railway's
incursion into England had ended. Devoid of any maintenance the Solway

Viaduct slowly deteriorated until it was
demolished in 1933, in the intervening
years used by foolhardy Scottish locals
desperate to have an alcoholic bevvy
in England when their own pubs were
closed on a Sunday night.

Despite the long passage of time there
are still reminders of the viaduct to be
seen today on the Cumbrian shore. Here,
there are a few rusting cast-iron piers on
the shoreline along with the remains of
the embankment on Bowness Common
which now forms part of English
Nature's Solway Basin Nature Reserve.

IN THE NEWS

Selective Scheduling Of Express Trains

We are reminded by certain of the train alterations that come into effect on 1 December of the increasing extent to which express trains are scheduled publicly so as to omit apparently vital stations. In these days of fully loaded trains and heavy traffic between certain trading and industrial centres, time-table peculiarities of this character may be looked for in an increasing degree, and it is possible that, in time to come, we shall get used to seeing trains apparently advertised non-stop from Newcastle to Peterborough, London to Carlisle or Holyhead, and even London to Edinburgh or Glasgow.

A Roof Over Our Heads

An innovative housing scheme by the London & North Western Railway

[Following the end of the Great War there was a general shortage of houses in Britain. This exacerbated labour difficulties for large employers such as the London & North Western Railway.] To alleviate this problem the company is embarking on a housing scheme of its own. Fifty wooden huts of the army type are to be erected at Crewe, adjacent to the public park which the company presented to the town on a former occasion. Each hut will be thoroughly damp proof, being supported on brick foundations, and will include three bedrooms, sitting room, kitchen and bathroom. The huts are to be laid out on the lines of a garden city with a large recreational space in the centre. The work is being carried out by the LNWR's own employees and it is hoped to have all 50 homes finished within a few months. If this is the case then a railway company will have the credit of putting up a larger number of houses in a shorter time since the armistice than any local authority or private builder.

.... November 1919

Light Railway Schemes In Shropshire

Various proposals for light railway schemes have recently been put forward in Shropshire. One scheme is for a railway to link Bishop's Castle, which is the present terminus of the Craven Arms to Bishop's Castle Railway, with the Cambrian Railways somewhere in the vicinity of Montgomery, but going via Chirbury. The distance is 12 miles, and the route presents no engineering difficulties. Other schemes include a railway from the Joint Railways at Craven Arms by way of Corvedale, 20 miles to Bridgnorth, and thence 15 miles to Wolverhampton, and a railway from Craven Arms to Newcastle, in the Clun Forest area, a distance of 12 miles.

FOOTNOTE: If all of these lines had been built then sleepy Craven Arms would have become the 'Crewe' of Shropshire.

Great Northern Railway Literary Society

The 29th Annual Smoking Concert of the Great Northern Railway Literary Society was held at the Queen's Hall on November 21. Lieut.-Col. The Hon. F.S. Jackson, M.P. (director of the Great Northern Railway), presided over a large gathering. The following officers of the company were present:- Mr C.H. Dent (General Manager), Mr E.H. Burrows (Secretary), Mr H.N.Gresley (Locomotive Engineer) ……………..The large audience thoroughly appreciated the excellent programme provided, and demands for encores were very numerous.

FOOTNOTE: Smoking concerts were live performances, usually of music, that were performed before a men-only audience. They became popular in the Victorian era and were social occasions where men would smoke and talk politics while listening to the music.

STEAM DREAMS
Reliving steam-hauled journeys of the '60s

Carlisle to Glasgow Central

Passengers on the down 'Royal Scot' on the 1 August 1964 were none too pleased when their English Electric Type 4 diesel failed as the train arrived at Carlisle. They probably didn't notice two excited teenage boys boarding the train as the diesel was taken off and replaced by a rather grimy BR Standard Class 7MT 4-6-2 No. 70002 'Geoffrey Chaucer'.

As it was a Saturday the express should have left Carlisle at 4.07pm but eventually left for its journey north at 4.32pm. Poor old 'Geoffrey Chaucer' really wasn't up to the task but our two trainspotters faithfully recorded every bit of the journey in their notebooks, spending most of the journey with their heads out of the window!

The first part of the journey up Annandale was excruciatingly slow: Quintinshill, Kirtlebridge and Ecclefechan all being passed at a measly 36mph; Lockerbie was passed at 63mph before we made an unscheduled stop at Beattock at 5.34pm to attach a banking engine. So far we had covered 39½ miles in 62 minutes – some express! After a 3½-minute stop at Beattock we were off again, breasting the summit at 6.01pm at a speed of 30mph. From then on it was all downhill and 'Geoffrey Chaucer' did his best to speed things up a bit along the Clyde Valley: Elvanfoot was passed at 69mph; Crawford and Abington at 72, Lamington at 70 before slowing for Carstairs (6.25pm) which we passed at 35mph. Speed slowly picked up again with a maximum of 65mph recorded at Carluke (6.36pm) and 63 at Shieldmuir Junction. Glasgow Central was reached at 7pm – exactly one hour late. The passengers were pretty fed up but the two trainspotters were ecstatic. Obviously in poor condition, 'Geoffrey Chaucer' and his crew had done their best, covering the 102¼ miles in 2hrs 28min at an average speed of 41.39mph. Now the Pendolinos only take around 1hr 15min at an average speed of nearly 82mph, progress indeed – but I would rather arrive one hour late behind a steam loco.

FOOTNOTE: 'Geoffrey Chaucer' was finally withdrawn from Carlisle Kingmoor shed in January 1967 and sent to the great steam scrapheap in the sky.

Aberdeen to Glasgow Buchanan Street

Our intrepid trainspotters had caught the 8.25am three-hour express (aka 'The Grampian') from Glasgow Buchanan Street to Aberdeen on 31 July 1964. Sadly the hoped-for 'A4' didn't materialise and we had to be content with Birmingham Railway Carriage & Wagon Co. Type 2 D5368. After a trawl around Ferryhill (all steam including seven 'A4s') and Kittybrewster (all diesels

apart from stored No. 60007) we returned on the 1.30pm to Glasgow Buchanan Street, supposedly the up 'The Grampian' express but in reality a stopping train taking four hours for the 153-mile journey via Forfar.

At the head of our train was 'A4' 4-6-2 No. 60019 'Bittern' which, despite the numerous stops along the way, managed to achieve some reasonable speeds: 72mph between Aberdeen and Stonehaven; 70 between Stonehaven and

Laurencekirk; 66 between Laurencekirk and Bridge of Dun; 65 between Bridge of Dun and Forfar; 73 between Forfar and Coupar Angus; 73 between Coupar Angus and Perth; 64 between Perth and Gleneagles; 66 between Gleneagles and Dunblane; 78 between Dunblane and Stirling; 78 between Stirling and Larbert.

FOOTNOTE: Our trainspotters were also lucky to have a ride behind No. 60024 'Kingfisher' between Stirling and Buchanan Street on 23 August 1966, just before the end of the 'A4s' swan song on this route. Happy days!

Banbury to Oxford

The York to Bournemouth through train was an interesting working, travelling via the Great Central line through Woodford Halse and Banbury. Here, on a sunny 9 September 1965 our two trainspotters boarded the train for the journey down to Oxford. We were lucky indeed as, although the reign of steam on the Western Region was due to end in just under four months, our train engine which came on at Banbury was 'Hall' Class 4-6-0 No. 4920 (formerly 'Dumbleton Hall' but by then minus its valuable nameplates) of Bristol (Barrow Road) shed.

Our train left Banbury at 2.42pm, passing King's Sutton at 2.50, Aynho at 2.53 and reaching 60mph at Fritwell which was passed at 2.56pm. Unfortunately the train was halted by signals at Heyford for nine minutes but put on a good spurt of speed reaching 64mph between Bletchington and Kidlington which was passed at 3.18pm. Wolvercote Junction was passed at 59 mph and we came to a screeching halt at Oxford station at 3.25pm where the Bournemouth to York train was seen heading northbound behind 'Modified Hall' 4-6-0 No. 7912 'Little Linford Hall'.

FOOTNOTE: This was the author's last journey behind an ex-GWR loco before the end of steam on BR. Luckily, 'Dumbleton Hall' survived withdrawal at the end of 1965 and was saved for preservation after having spent over 10 years at Woodham's scrapyard in Barry.

A METROPOLITAN TRAIN

STOP PRESS
Railway news, July 1928

The LNER recently completed the placing of the orders for their new fleet of 50 Sentinel-Cammell and Clayton rail coaches that are to be used at various points of the system, principally where intense services are required for special purposes in districts that are not yet ripe for development on ordinary lines. One of the most interesting features of the introduction of these coaches is that each is being named after one of the famous road stage coaches of early days. The following are some of the names that have already been allotted: 'Tally Ho'; 'Highflyer'; 'Hero'; 'True Briton'; 'Teazle'; 'True Blue'; 'Bang Up'; 'Chevy Chase'.

One of the latest type of LMS 2-6-4 passenger tank locomotive of the '2300' Class now bears the name 'The Prince' on its side tanks. The engine in question, No. 2313, was inspected by the Prince of Wales upon the occasion of his recent visit to Derby. No. 2313 is painted in the new standard black livery with red lining, and is working with seven others of this class in the Manchester area. This is the only instance of a named tank locomotive on the LMS and it is not intended to name the other engines of the same class.

One of the latest 2-6-0 class of LMS locomotives runs to Fleetwood daily from Manchester, and at present has to run light for no fewer than 10 miles in order to turn for the return journey. As there is no turntable at Fleetwood long enough, the 'Mogul', after its train is shunted out of the terminus by another engine, runs backward to Poulton Junction, traverses the loop line at that point, and returns to Fleetwood tender first again, a total distance of 10 miles.

Brief details were given earlier this year for a proposed electric underground railway for Manchester that for some time past has been occupying the attention of a special committee of the Manchester Corporation. An alternative scheme has now been presented for consideration. This provides for the construction of an inner circular railway linking the chief railway stations in the city.

In the middle of April trials were conducted on the LMS railway between Manchester and Blackpool with a diesel-electric train, the first of its kind seen in Great Britain. The power unit is built into the leading coach and consists of a 500hp Beardmore diesel engine driving electric generators which, in turn, supply power to the traction motors. The engine is run on crude oil and a train of average weight can be hauled at a speed of from 50 to 55 mph. The leading coach was built by the English Electric Company, Preston.

The London, Midland & Scottish Railway has recently set a new world record for the world's longest non-stop railway run. On 27 April, the necessity for running the 'Royal Scot' in duplicate arose, and separate portions for Edinburgh and Glasgow, respectively 399¾ and 401½ miles from Euston, were put on. Each accomplished its journey without a halt. The Edinburgh train was worked by a 4-4-0 compound and the Glasgow train by a 'Royal Scot'. Each engine having a crew of two drivers and one fireman.

TICKETS PLEASE!
The story of railway-owned road motor services

With the advent of the internal combustion engine, railway companies were quick to realise that the cost of running a motor bus service in sparsely populated areas was cheaper than building a railway. Despite the GWR being given the credit for the introduction of railway bus services it was the narrow gauge Lynton & Barnstaple Railway (L&BR) that led the way, albeit for a very brief period.

By the beginning of the 20th century the hilly omnibus route between Ilfracombe and Lynton was heavily used during the summer months and was a lucrative market that the L&BR aimed to capture. In 1903, Sir George Newnes, the principal financier of the railway, set about buying two motor coaches which would run from Ilfracombe to Blackmoor Gate station where passengers would transfer on to the railway for the journey to Lynton. This

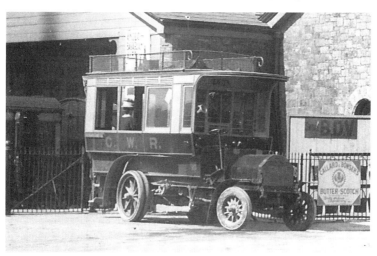

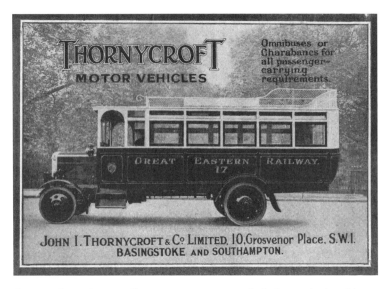

first experiment by any railway to run a motor coach feeder service lasted less than one season mainly due to the bus drivers being fined for speeding by the local police. The motor coaches were then sold to the GWR for their new Helston to The Lizard Route.

The pioneer of regular railway feeder bus services, the GWR had already opened its branch line from Gwinear Road to Helston in 1887. Before long there were demands for a light railway to be built from Helston down to The Lizard but the cost was prohibitive for such a sparsely populated part of Cornwall so the company decided to experiment with a bus service. Using the two buses previously owned by the Lynton & Barnstaple Railway the new service proved both popular and profitable and within a couple of years the GWR had introduced rail motor services all over its system – Cornwall, Devon, the Cotswolds, Somerset, the Thames Valley, the Midlands and Wales. By the end of 1904 the company had 36 buses operating, some of which were steam powered.

The legality of the GWR's bus services was doubtful until the Great Western Railway (Road Transport) Act was passed in 1928 by which time the company owned the largest railway-operated bus fleet in the country. Many routes were soon transferred to nominally independent bus companies but in reality these were still part-owned by the GWR – for example all routes in Devon and Cornwall were transferred to the Western National Omnibus Company at the beginning of 1929, but this was still half-owned by the railway.

Other railway companies around the country also introduced their own bus services; notable among them was the Great North of Scotland Railway, the London & North Western Railway and the Great Eastern Railway.

Great North of Scotland Railway bus routes

The GNoSR was also quick off the mark with a network of feeder bus services starting in 1904. By 1930, under LNER management, those routes remaining were sold off to private bus companies.

Ballater to Braemar (16½ miles) 1904-1930

Udny to Methlick (10¼ miles) 1904-1907

Huntly to Aberchirder (11¾ miles) 1905-1928 (extended to Banff 1928-1930)

Culter to Midmar (12½ miles) 1905-1906

Alford to Cockbridge (27¾ miles) 1906-1929

Aberdeen to Cluny (16½ miles) 1906-1922

Aberdeen to Newburgh (14¾ miles) 1907-1922

Ballindalloch to Tomintoul (15¾ miles) Summer only 1910-1925

Ballater to Cockbridge (29 miles) Summer only 1907-1925

Fraserburgh to New Aberdour (9½ miles) 1912-1927

Aberchirder to Turriff (7¼ miles) Summer only 1921

Aberchirder to Banff (20 miles) 1928-1930

Aberdeen to Inverurie (15¾ miles) 1927-1930

Aberdeen to Strathdon via Alford (47½ miles) 1929-1930

Elgin to Macduff (35¾ miles) 1929-1930

Aberdeen to Ballater (40¼ miles) 1929-1930

CHIP VANS
The story of Sentinel Steam Railcars

B uilders of steam railcars in the early 20th century, the Sentinel Waggon Works started life in Glasgow in 1875 as Alley & MacLellan. Here they produced steam road vehicles but also boats. The company moved its steam road vehicle production to a new factory in Shrewsbury in 1915 and was taken over by William Beardmore & Co two years later.

In addition to building geared steam locomotives for the LMS, LNER and the Somerset & Dorset Joint Railway, the company supplied a large number of steam railcars, the first to the narrow gauge Jersey Railway in 1923. The majority were built mainly for the LNER but also one for the Axholme Joint Railway, one for the Southern Railway, one for New Zealand Railways and ten for Egyptian National Railways. In 1959 the company started to build diesel locomotives, culminating in Rolls-Royce-engined diesels for use in steel works – these later saw life as a replacement for the Class 14 diesels on British Railways.

By far the largest order of steam railcars were the 80 bought by the LNER between 1925 and 1932. Exhibited at the 1924 British Empire Exhibition, Sentinel's first standard gauge steam railcar was loaned to the LNER for trials in north-east England. Competing with an Armstrong-Whitworth diesel-electric railcar the Sentinel steam railcar won the day and the success of these trials led to an order for 80 for use on the LNER and for four for the LNER-controlled Cheshire Lines Committee.

With bodywork built by Cammell Laird, Sentinel's steam railcars were self-contained vehicles with the boiler and driving compartment at the front followed by a luggage compartment and seating for 48-64 passengers, depending on model. At the other end was a remotely-operated driver's compartment for use when running backwards. Delivered between 1925 and 1932, eight different versions were built, some with vertical boilers while others had horizontal boilers. The earlier versions were chain driven but breakage problems with these led to the introduction of gear-driven versions. Two types were built with an articulated trailer car, while one, built in 1930, came as a twin car. The later versions were capable of speeds in excess of 60mph.

The Sentinel steam railcars, the majority of them receiving the names of famous stage coaches, were seen at work all over the LNER system, mainly on light branch lines but also on short suburban routes. By 1931, 15 had been allocated to Scotland with one being used for a short period out of Aberdeen Kittybrewster shed for service on ex-GNoSR branches. The confined space of the main driving compartment and their temperamental behaviour made them unpopular with their

NEW SUNDAY SERVICE

COMMENCING 8th MAY

		a.m.	p.m.
Wigan (Central)	... dep.	6.45	4. 0
Lower Ince	... ,,	6.48	4. 3
Hindley and Platt Bridge	,,	6.52	4. 7
Irlam and Cadishead	... arr.	7.12	4.27
		a.m.	p.m.
Irlam and Cadishead	... dep.	7.45	5.52
Hindley and Platt Bridge	,,	8. 4	6.12
Lower Ince	... ,,	8. 8	6.16
Wigan (Central)	... arr.	8.11	6.19

STEAM RAIL CAR

(ONE CLASS ONLY)

London, April, 1932.

L·N·E·R

crews – their box-like appearance and their smoking chimneys soon led to their nickname of 'Chip Vans'. Problems with maintenance eventually led to their demise and the last one, LNER No. 2136 'Hope', just survived into the British Railways era before withdrawal in February 1948.

Four steam railcars were also supplied to the Cheshire Lines Committee and one to the Southern Railway for use on the Brighton to Devil's Dyke branch. None of the British railcars survived but one articulated example from the ten supplied in 1951 to Egyptian National Railways has been preserved at the Buckinghamshire Railway Centre at Quainton Road.

THE 'TIDDLEY DYKE'
The story of the Midland & South Western Junction Railway

A ffectionately known as the 'Tiddley Dyke', the Midland & South Western Junction Railway was formed in 1884 by the amalgamation of two existing railway companies – the Swindon, Marlborough & Andover Railway and the Swindon & Cheltenham Extension Railway.

However, nearly 40 years previously, a proposal for the grandly named Manchester & Southampton Railway had been put before Parliament by the London & Birmingham Railway. With its chief engineer Robert Stephenson, the L&BR saw this new railway as an important north-south artery leaving the Midland Railway's Bristol to Birmingham mainline at Cheltenham and joining the London & South Western Railway at Romsey. Despite the backing of the Midland Railway and the London & Birmingham Railway and progressing through two sessions of Parliament the proposal was eventually thrown out in 1848.

Another 36 years elapsed before the southern section of what later became the M&SWJR opened for business. This was the single track Swindon, Marlborough & Andover Railway (SM&AR) which opened throughout (apart from Grafton to Marlborough) between Red Posts Junction at Andover and Rushey Platt at Swindon in 1884. However, there was a little difficulty at Marlborough as the missing link between Grafton and the town failed to be built due to a shortage of funds. Until 1898 trains had to travel via a short link with the GWR's branch from Savernake which had already opened in 1862 – the GWR insisted that passengers wanting to change at Savernake had to use GWR trains from Marlborough!

To the north of Swindon the single track Swindon & Cheltenham Extension Railway was authorised in 1881. However, only the section from Rushey Platt to Cirencester (Watermoor) had been completed by 1883 when the company ran into financial difficulties. A year later the company amalgamated with the SM&AR to form the Midland & South

Western Junction Railway – the missing link northwards from Cirencester to Andoversford was completed in 1891. At the northern end the M&SWJR had obtained running rights over the GWR's Cheltenham to Kingham line between Andoversford and Banbury Line Junction at Cheltenham. Here their trains terminated at the Midland Railway's Lansdown station.

Now more or less complete but nearly bankrupt and in the hands of a receiver, the M&SWJR was saved from oblivion when Sam Fay, seconded by the London & South Western Railway, was appointed Secretary and General Manager in 1892. During his seven-year tenure Fay turned the ailing M&SWJR into a thriving concern, opening a locomotive, carriage and wagon repair works at Cirencester, completing the missing link between Grafton and Marlborough and obtaining running powers over the LSWR's 'Sprat & Winkle Line' between Andover and Redbridge. By the time Fay had left in 1899 (soon to become General Manager of the Great Central Railway) trains could travel from the North and Midlands over Midland Railway metals to

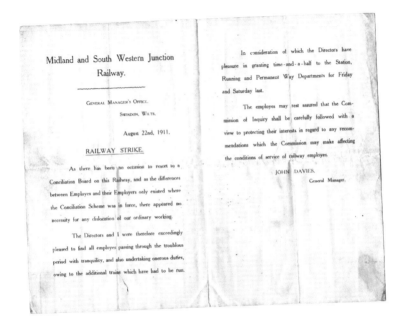

Midland and South Western Junction
Railway.

GENERAL MANAGER'S OFFICE.

SWINDON, WILTS.

August 22nd, 1911.

RAILWAY STRIKE.

As there has been no occasion to resort to a
Conciliation Board on this Railway, and as the differences
between Employes and their Employers only existed where
the Conciliation Scheme was in force, there appeared no
necessity for any dislocation of our ordinary working.

The Directors and I were therefore exceedingly
pleased to find all employes passing through the troublous
period with tranquility, and also undertaking onerous duties,
owing to the additional trains which have had to be run.

In consideration of which the Directors have
pleasure in granting time-and-a-half to the Station,
Running and Permanent Way Departments for Friday
and Saturday last.

The employes may rest assured that the Commission of Inquiry shall be carefully followed with a
view to protecting their interests in regard to any recom-
mendations which the Commission may make affecting
the conditions of service of railway employes.

JOHN DAVIES,

General Manager.

Cheltenham then via the M&SWJR and the LSWR to Southampton – one
weekday train which carried through carriages between Liverpool Lime Street
and Southampton travelled via the M&SWJR, although the total journey time
of 7hrs 10min via this meandering north–south route must have been tedious
for passengers.

Providing a link between military centres such as Tidworth and Ludgershall
on Salisbury Plain and Southampton Docks, the M&SWJR naturally saw
heavy use during the South African Wars and World War I. Racehorse traffic
in the Marlborough area, milk traffic north of Swindon and pigeon trains
from the North were also important in the railway's early years. However,
at the Big Four Grouping of 1923, the M&SWJR became part of the Great
Western Railway. The company's 29 locomotives, products of Dübs, Sharp

Stewart and Beyer Peacock, were 'Swindonised', three 2-4-0s even surviving into the British Railways era. By the 1950s services had become very reduced with only one through train each weekday running between Cheltenham Lansdown and Southampton Central, the 94½-mile journey taking around four hours to complete. In 1958 this train was diverted to run into Cheltenham (St James) station (the option for changing trains at Lansdown was now lost) and the regular but unusual sight of a SR 'Mogul' and its short train of SR green carriages at the station can be well remembered by the author. By then the writing was on the wall for this delightful rural line and it closed on 10 September 1961.

Despite closure 50 years ago parts of the M&SWJR live on:

The Swindon & Cricklade Railway now operates steam trains along a mile of track each side of Blunsdon station, north of Swindon.

Much of the trackbed between Cricklade and Marlborough is now a footpath and cyclway forming part of National Cycle Network Route 45.

The section of line between Red Posts Junction at Andover and Ludgershall remains open for military traffic to Tidworth Camp.

NEW FOR OLD
Extinct classes of steam locos that are now being reborn

Despite the efforts of preservationists and the treasure trove of Dai Woodham's scrapyard in Barry many classes of steam locomotive had become extinct over 40 years ago. Following the success of the brand new Peppercorn Class 'A1' 4-6-2 'Tornado', other classes are now in the process of being built as new.

LNER Peppercorn Class A1 4-62 No. 60163 'Tornado'
Once a regular sight on East Coast main line expresses, the 49 'A1' locos designed by Arthur Peppercorn and introduced in 1948-49 had a short working life on average of only 15 years. Five of the class (Nos. 60153-60157) were fitted

with Timken roller bearings and these proved to be the most reliable British steam locos ever built, managing around 120,000 miles between each works' overhaul. Despite this they had arrived on the scene too late and had all been withdrawn by 1966. No. 60145 'St Mungo' was the last to be withdrawn in June of that year and despite valiant attempts to save her from the scrapheap the rescue effort was unsuccessful.

Fast forward to 1990 when a group of engineers and enthusiasts founded the 'A1 Steam Locomotive Trust'. Their aim was to build a brand new Class 'A1' incorporating many modern improvements; £3 million and 18 years later No. 60163 emerged under her own steam from her birthplace at Darlington Locomotive Works. Following a period of running-in on the Great Central Railway this magnificent locomotive, resplendent in apple green livery, was named 'Tornado' by the Prince of Wales at York station in February 2009. With a ten-year boiler certificate and capable of running at 100mph, the loco has already put in many fine performances on the main line and has drawn crowds wherever she appears.

GWR Hawksworth 'County' Class 4-6-0 No. 1014 'County of Glamorgan'

Designed by Frederick Hawksworth, 30 'County' Class locos were built at Swindon Works between 1945 and 1947. Based on Hawksworth's successful 'Modified Hall' Class locos and incorporating a number of new technological improvements they were seen as a precursor to a new 'Pacific' 4-6-2 design. The latter never materialised and the 'Counties' had short working lives with the last member, No. 1011 'County of Chester', being withdrawn in September 1964. The majority of the class were scrapped at Cashmore's in Newport and none was preserved.

Since December 2004 members of the Great Western Society at Didcot have been recreating one of these fine locos using the underframes from 'Modified Hall' Class 4-6-0 No. 7927 'Willington Hall' and a rebuilt boiler from Stanier 8F 2-8-0 No. 48518 – both these locos had previously been purchased from Woodham's scrapyard at Barry. Despite this and the donation of various parts (including the double chimney from No. 1006) from scrapped 'Counties', much of the locomotive along with the flat-sided Hawksworth tender will have to be built from scratch. It will probably be a few more years until we see No. 1014 in steam on the main line.

GWR Churchward 'Saint' Class 4-6-0 No. 2999 'Lady of Legend'

A total of 76 of the 'Saint' Class locos were built at Swindon between 1902 and 1913. They had all been withdrawn by 1953 but one, No. 2925

'Saint Martin', was rebuilt as the prototype 'Hall' Class loco, No. 4900. Today, members of the Great Western Society at Didcot are recreating a 'Saint' Class loco by rebuilding Hall Class 4-6-0 No. 4942 'Maindy Hall'. The latter loco was withdrawn at the end of 1963 and spent 11 years rusting at Woodham's scrapyard in Barry before being purchased by the Great Western Society. Work is now well underway at Didcot and it shouldn't be too long before the new 'Lady of Legend' is back on the main line.

GWR Steam Railmotor No. 93
Seen at work all over the GWR system, the humble steam railmotor was the precursor to the steam autotrain and diesel railcars so beloved of that company. Powered by a steam–driven bogie these self-propelled carriages were introduced in 1903 and were phased out in the 1930s with the introduction of autotrains – many of the railmotor coaches were rebuilt for use as autotrains which continued in use, usually powered by '1400' Class 0-4-2 tanks, until 1964.

Fortunately the Great Western Society at Didcot bought autotrain coach No. 212 in the early 1970s. This had been rebuilt from the original steam railmotor No. 93 in the 1930s and, together with auto trailer No. 92, offered the chance to return it to its original working condition. Today, assisted by a £768,500 grant from the Heritage Lottery Fund, work has been completed on the restoration of Railmotor No. 93 and trailer No. 92 in the workshops of the Llangollen Railway and it returned to steam in 2011.

GWR 'Grange' Class 4-6-0 No. 6880 'Betton Grange'
Built at Swindon between 1936 and 1939 the 80 'Grange' Class locos were rebuilds of earlier '4300' Class 2-6-0s (as were 20 of the 'Manor' Class). They were successful mixed traffic locos that had all been withdrawn by December 1965. None of this class was preserved.

Formed in 1998, the '6880 Society' is currently building the 81st 'Grange' at Llangollen Railway Works. It will carry the number 6880 and will be named 'Betton Grange'. The front bogie and tender from 'Hall' Class 4-6-0 No. 5952

'Cogan Hall', saved from Woodham's scrapyard in 1981, are being used in the construction of the new loco.

Unrebuilt LMS Fowler 'Patriot' Class 4-6-0 No. 45551 'The Unknown Warrior'

Designed by Sir Henry Fowler, 52 'Patriot' Class locos (known as 'Baby Scots') were built with parallel boilers between 1930 and 1934. Subsequently 18 were rebuilt with tapered boilers between 1946 and 1949. All of the class, both unrebuilt and rebuilt, had been withdrawn by the end of 1965 and none were saved for preservation.

Today the LMS-Patriot Project has started construction of a brand new parallel boiler unrebuilt loco of this class. Using original LMS drawings, work on the project has already started at the Llangollen Railway Works and apart from the frames and wheelsets of an existing Fowler tender all other parts will have to be built from scratch. The cost of this will be in the region of £1.5 million so it will be some years before we see this loco in steam.

Streamlined LMS 'Coronation' Class 4-6-2 No. 46229 'Duchess of Hamilton'

While not a totally new locomotive, LMS 'Coronation' Class 4-6-2 No. 46229 'Duchess of Hamilton' has recently been given a new streamlined casing and has pride of place at the National Railway Museum in York. The loco was originally built at Crewe with a streamlined casing in 1938 but this was removed, as with other members of this class, in 1947. The loco also appeared at the 1939 New York World's Fair in 1939 masquerading as No. 6220 'Coronation'. Although withdrawn in 1964 this fine loco was saved for preservation (thanks initially to Sir Billy Butlin) and has since seen many years of mainline operations. A new streamlined casing was reinstated at Tyseley Locomotive Works and the loco returned to York in 2009. Perhaps, one day in the future, we may see this iconic loco back at work on the main line again.

BR Standard 'Clan' Class 6MT 4-6-2·No. 72010 'Hengist'

British Railways originally planned to build 118 Class 6MT 'Clan' 4-6-2s but, due to a severe steel shortage in 1954, production was cut short. In the end only ten were built for use in Scotland between 1951 and 1952, all of which were named after Scottish clans. The last surviving member of the class, No. 72008 'Clan MacLeod' was withdrawn in April 1966. No members of the class were preserved.

If the 'Clan' production line hadn't been stopped the next loco to have been built (for the Southern Region) would have been No. 72010 'Hengist'. Formed in 1993, the Standard Steam Locomotive Company is currently building a brand new 'Hengist' and to date has spent around £1 million on the project. The company is also looking for a base from which they can complete the loco.

GHOST TRAINS

The countdown to Britain's Bottom 20 least used stations calculated by total entries and exits during 2008/9.

19= Falls of Cruachan, Highland – 218

Served by trains on Glasgow to Oban line. Closed in 1965, reopened in 1988 for visitors to Cruachan hydro-electric power station and for climbers of Ben Cruachan.

19= Lochluichart, Highland – 218

Served by trains on Inverness to Kyle of Lochalsh line.

17= Clifton, Greater Manchester – 216

On Manchester to Preston line. One train in each direction on weekdays.

17= Polesworth, Warwickshire – 216

On Trent Valley section of West Coast main line. Only one northbound train on weekdays.

16 Rawcliffe, East Yorkshire – 204

On Pontefract to Goole line. One train each weekday in easterly direction, two trains each weekday in westerly direction.

15 Beasdale, Highland – 200

Served by trains on Fort William to Mallaig line.

14 Chapelton, Devon – 176

Served by trains on Exeter to Barnstaple line.

13 Kildonan, Highland – 174

Served by trains on Inverness to Wick/Thurso line.

12 Elton & Orston, Nottinghamsire – 172

On Nottingham to Skegness line. One train on weekdays in each direction.

11 Golf Street, Carnoustie, Angus – 136
On Dundee to Aberdeen main line. One train each weekday in each direction.

10 Buckenham, Norfolk – 132
On Norwich to Yarmouth/Lowestoft line (via Reedham Junction). Used by birdwatchers visiting nearby RSPB reserve. Four trains in each direction on Sundays, one train on Saturdays in each direction.

9 Pilning, South Gloucestershire – 130
On Bristol to South Wales main line to the east of the Severn Tunnel. One train on Saturdays in each direction.

8 Sugar Loaf, Powys – 120
The least used station in Wales. Located at the north end of Sugar Loaf Tunnel and served by trains on the Central Wales line. Used mainly by walkers.

7 Coombe Junction Halt – 118
On Liskeard to Looe branch line. Served by two trains each weekday in each direction despite all passenger trains needing to reverse at the nearby junction before continuing their journey.

6 Dorking West, Surrey – 104★
On Guildford to Redhill line. Served by a two-hourly train service on weekdays in each direction.

5 Barry Links, Carnoustie, Angus – 94
The least used station in Scotland. On Dundee to Aberdeen main line. One train each weekday in each direction.

4 Kirton Lindsey, North Lincolnshire – 88
On Gainsborough to Barnetby line. Served by three trains in each direction on Saturdays only.

3 Maidstone Barracks, Kent – 70★
On the Paddock Wood to Strood line with regular hourly trains.

2 Denton, Greater Manchester – 56

On Stalybridge to Stockport line via Reddish South. Served by one train each week in one direction only.

1 Tees-side Airport, County Durham – 44

Located some distance from the airport it purports to serve on the Darlington to Middlesbrough line. The least used station in the UK, served by one train in each direction on Saturdays only.

FOOTNOTES: Many of these stations are being closed by stealth with some only receiving one train each week. The token services offered are known as Parliamentary trains which are only provided to get round formal closure procedures as the line or station is still technically open. Ticket numbers for some of these 'ghost stations' are probably swelled by collectors of the unusual! Other Parliamentary trains that keep open 'ghost lines' include a Chester to Runcorn train that operates only on Saturdays in the summer, one weekday train between Lancaster and Windermere via Morecambe and between Ellesmere Port and Warrington. Some Parliamentary trains have even been replaced by a bus service that still calls at the stations – examples include the service between Rickmansworth and Watford and the infamous Ealing Broadway to Wandsworth Road once-a-week service. The Bristol to Severn Beach line is often closed beyond Avonmouth with trains being replaced by buses – perhaps this is another example of closure by stealth?

BRAIN TEASER: How many days would it take to travel by rail from Denton station in Greater Manchester to Tees-side Airport station in County Durham?

*These figures are suspect as there are two other stations in both Dorking and Maidstone. Passengers who may have booked to 'Dorking' or 'Maidstone' may well be alighting or joining at these two stations which are not so underused as they appear in the official figures.

NB The busiest station in Britain is London Waterloo with 87,930,076 entries and exits in 2008/9.

DOING IT LEGALLY
Engine shed, locomotive works and lineside permits

During the 1950s and early '60s it was considered rather a 'cissy' thing to apply for a permit to visit an engine shed! 'Shed bashing', as it was known, was a term used by trainspotters to describe their frenetic trips to as many engine sheds (usually without permits) as was possible in one day. Without an official permit some sheds were easier to visit than others depending on the friendliness of the shed foreman or the deviousness of the trainspotter. All manner of tricks were employed to gain access to the hallowed ground and once inside it was often a game of cat and mouse before we were eventually thrown out.

However, many visits were official and highly organised by the myriad railway societies up and down the country whose members were whisked from shed to shed by the coach load. It was a sad fact that many of these trips had to be made by road but (a) the trips were usually held on Sundays when the sheds were full and, because it was the Sabbath, there was only a limited or non-existent train service to the nearest station, and (b) there was no other practical way to visit such a large number of sheds in one day as many of them were located on out-of-the-way goods-only lines. Naturally, the proper paperwork had been done by the society and the necessary permits obtained.

The Stoke Division of the LMR issued detailed conditions for visits to their engine sheds including the stipulation that visitors must travel by rail! No wonder so many trainspotters 'bunked' sheds without permission. Prior notification also had to be given if any females wished to travel with the

party! There was also a stipulation that any photographs taken were for private collection only – this latter stipulation was obviously not enforced.

Visits to railway works were also often made on Sundays when the work force was at home digging the garden or out ferreting. Annual open days, at Crewe, Derby and Swindon for instance also, drew large crowds of spotters. To

accommodate the young trainspotter Swindon Works also allowed visits without a permit on a Wednesday afternoon during the school holidays.

Lineside passes for photographers were much harder to come by and only the 'chosen few' responsible adults (or BR employees) were handed one of these!

EVENIN' ALL!
The story of the railway policeman

Known since 1949 as the British Transport Police, the first railway policemen in Britain were employed by the Liverpool & Manchester Railway to keep order when it opened in 1830. Even before this men were employed in the capacity of unofficial special constables to control the often unruly navvies who were building the railways – these so-called policemen were actually chosen from among the navvies themselves, in reality a form of self-policing. Soon thousands of these construction workers (most of them from the Emerald Isle) were swarming over England's green and pleasant land, often creating mayhem in previously peaceful areas. The 1838 Special Constables Act set out to address this problem by forcing the railway companies and their contractors to fund policing around construction sites – the Act's full title was appropriately worded: 'An Act for the Payment of Constables for keeping the Peace near Public Works'.

Once the railways were open police were also needed to protect property and passengers – one of the earliest of these railway policemen was Constable John Metcalfe who was appointed by the Stockton & Darlington Railway in 1846. His portrait now hangs in the National Railway Museum, York.

The GWR was one of the first railway companies granted powers to appoint police – the Great Western Railway Act of 1835 contained provisions for constables to be appointed, but only on its premises. It wasn't until 1877 that they were given powers to operate further afield. In the meantime the railway policeman had to deal with not only a whole range of crimes, from drunkenness and smoking (the latter prohibited on all railway premises and in trains until 1868 when smoking carriages were introduced) to robbery and murder, but also the control of trains and to clear the line of obstructions. In the early years of the London & Birmingham Railway constables were placed about a mile apart along the whole length of the line as signalmen, armed with coloured flags for daytime use and lamps for the night time. On the GWR a

policeman was located on average every 1½ miles along the track, housed in wooden shelters at the lineside and required to salute each train as it passed.

Railway employees could also be sworn in as special constables in times of trouble, for instance during the threatened Chartists' riots in 1848 when 20,000 special constables were put on alert by the London & North Western Railway.

The fast expanding railway network in Britain was a golden opportunity for criminals, enabling them to move quickly around the country, committing crime and avoiding detection. The introduction of the lineside electric telegraph in 1843 (by the GWR between Paddington and Slough) soon brought dramatic results – on 1 January 1845 a murderer who boarded a train at Slough was apprehended in London after his details had been telegraphed along the line. The murderer, John Tawell, was later sentenced to death, becoming the first criminal in the world to be caught by electric telegraph.

By 1921 around 20 British railway companies had their own police force – the North Eastern Railway's police force was the first to introduce dogs in 1908 when they were used for patrolling Hull Docks. Until World War I railway constables were also employed to control horse-drawn cabs at London termini by a fee of one penny from those permitted to trade there.

Even from their early days the railways had become a honey-pot for criminals bent on robbing wagons and depots of their goods and passengers of their valuables, while the carrying of mail on trains also brought further ill-gotten gains. Parcels and mailbags left hanging around on station platforms were easy pickings and child delinquency in the form of stone throwing and placing obstacles on the line was rife. The railway policeman had his hands full!

The Grouping of 1923 saw the police forces of the four newly formed major railway companies receive extra powers including stop and search, and arrest of employees suspected of company theft. Following the nationalisation of the railways the British Transport Commission Act of 1949 led to the formation of the British Transport Police who were given wide-ranging powers not only on the railways but also on the canals and docks infrastructure around Britain. The BTP continues to this day, now funded mainly by the train operating companies, Network Rail and London Underground, and employs nearly 2,900 police officers along with several hundred special constables, police community support officers and a backroom staff of around 1,300. Their frontline 'police stations' can be found at 88 railway stations around the country.

FOOTNOTE: Everyone has heard of the 'Great Train Robbery' of 1963 when £2.6 million was stolen from a travelling post office train in Buckinghamshire but give a thought to the first major train robbery that happened in 1855 on the South Eastern Railway.

By the late 1840s gold bullion was regularly being carried by boat train from London to Folkestone on the first part of its journey to Paris. A certain Edward Agar hit on the bright idea of robbing one of these trains by availing himself of duplicate keys for the travelling safes and set about making friends with a SER boat train guard and the stationmaster of London Bridge station. After carrying out a successful dummy run in 1854, Agar, with prior knowledge of the weight of the gold consignment and the use of his duplicate keys, was able to swap £14,000 of bullion for the same weight in lead shot before the train arrived at Folkestone. The 'lead bullion' was taken out of the train Agar and his co-conspirator Edward Pierce stayed behind and left the train at Dover, returning to London with their ill-gotten gains.

There was uproar in Paris the next morning when the theft was discovered. In the end the French accused the British and vice versa but there were no clues on either side of the Channel as to how it had happened. The gold (at today's price worth around £1.1 million) was melted down by Agar and he nearly got away with it but for a twist of fate. Framed for forging a cheque by his new lover's ex-boy friend, Agar was sentenced to transportation to Australia for life. Meanwhile, Agar's previous lover, Fanny, was now getting pretty angry with Pierce who had been looking after some of the gold to care for her and her (also Agar's) child. Furious that the double-crossing Pierce wouldn't help her, she reported the whole sorry affair to the authorities – acting promptly they seized Agar from his prison ship in Portland Harbour just before it sailed to the Antipodes. In the subsequent trial Agar turned on his accomplices, two of whom were sentenced to transportation to Australia for 14 years while Pierce only received two years. What was left of the money was divided between the South Eastern Railway and the Police Chief with instructions that it be used to care for Fanny and her child.

ORDER! ORDER!
Railway questions in the House of Commons, November 1919

The Channel Tunnel

Sir Arthur Fell asked the Prime Minister if he could arrange for the Government to receive the advice of the War Office and Admiralty on the question of the Channel Tunnel in time to render the deposit of the Bill in Parliament this December possible, so that it might, if the standing orders were dispensed with, proceed next session and, if passed, save a whole year's time in the construction of the tunnel.

Mr Lloyd George: The War Office and the Admiralty are examining this question as quickly as possible, and I shall let my hon. friend know when I am in a position to answer his question.

Sir A. Fell: May we have some hope that this will be done in time to enable the Bill to be deposited in December this year?

Mr Lloyd George: I can quite see the force of my hon. friend's appeal, and I will certainly do what I can to have a decision in time to enable the promoters to give the necessary notice this year.

FOOTNOTE: Despite Sir Arthur Fell's insistence on speeding up the process it was another 75 years before the Channel Tunnel was built!

The price of coal

Sir R. Williams [Minister of Transport], replying to Mr Hartshorn, said that the amount allowed in the estimated expenditure of the railway companies for the present financial year in respect of the increase of 6s. per ton in the price of coal was approximately £3,000,000.

FOOTNOTE: At today's prices this would be approximately £114,000,000.

The carriage of hay

Sir E. Geddes, answering Mr. Brace, said: One complaint of delay in conveyance of hay to a South Wales colliery has been brought to my notice, but on inquiry the complaint was not substantiated. I am not aware of any special ground for complaint as regards this class of traffic, and regret I cannot support the suggestion that it should be included in the category of perishable foodstuffs.

FOOTNOTE: In 1913 there were 70,000 pit ponies working down coal mines in Britain and enormous amounts of hay, transported by rail, were required to keep them fed.

The shortage of wagons

Mr Royce asked the Minister of Transport whether he was aware that the shortage of railway trucks in South Lincolnshire and adjacent areas was causing discontent and loss to agriculturalists; whether he was aware that produce was often taken to a station five or six times and had to be returned owing to no trucks being available, involving many miles of cartage; whether this shortage of trucks was keeping up prices by preventing agricultural produce being put on the market; and whether he proposed to take steps to deal with this matter.

Sir R. Williams: I am not aware of any instances such as those referred to in the second part of his question, and there is a well-established custom under which farmers inquire whether trucks are available before carting their produce to the station. In view of the difficulties which traders experience in clearing wagons loaded with produce at London terminal stations, I do not think the shortage of trucks is keeping up the price of produce.

Sir R. Williams, in answer to Mr. Haydn Jones, said that the practice of loading private owners' wagons on the return journey when they would otherwise travel empty was in the public interest, in view of the present shortage of wagons.

FOOTNOTE: By this date, only a year after World War I had finished, there were still 19,000 goods wagons languishing in France which had been lent to the War Department by the railway companies. They were being returned to the UK at the rate of 520 per week.

BRUSH STROKES
Three notable railway poster artists

John Hassall (1868-1948)

John Hassall failed to enter the Royal Military Academy at Sandhurst so he emigrated to Canada in 1888 to farm with his brother. In 1890 he returned to London and had some of his drawings published in a magazine. He then went on to study art in Antwerp and Paris before returning to England in 1895 to begin work as an advertising artist for David Allen & Sons, the printing company that was to become famous for its London Transport posters. By 1900 Hassall had become a well-established illustrator, cartoonist and poster designer; his style of flat colours enclosed by black lines was also used as illustrations for children's books. His most famous work is the 'Jolly Fisherman' depicted on the 1908 Great Northern Railway's poster, 'Skegness is So Bracing', for which he received a fee of 12 guineas. Strangely he didn't visit the seaside resort until 1936 when he was given the 'freedom of the foreshore' and, despite his fame, he died penniless at the age of 80 years. Hassall's original Skegness masterpiece was presented to the town by British Railways in 1968 and now hangs in the Town Hall.

Norman Wilkinson (1878-1971)

Although receiving an early musical training, Wilkinson went on to study at Southsea School of Art and became an accomplished maritime artist, illustrator, poster artist and inventor of wartime camouflage. His illustration career started in 1898 with work for the *Illustrated London News* and he went on to design shipping posters for companies such as Cunard and a vast number of railway posters, firstly for the London & North Western Railway and then their successor, the LMS. During World War I he served with the Royal Naval Volunteer Reserve and hit upon the idea of camouflaging naval ships. His ideas were so successful that he led a team of camouflage artists in both World Wars and received an award for his invention of 'dazzle painting'.

As well as becoming one of the finest maritime painters of the 20th century (his painting, 'Plymouth Harbour', hung in the First Class smoking room of the 'Titanic'), Wilkinson is famous for his large-format landscape railway posters that adorned stations up and down the country. He even persuaded 17 Royal Academicians to produce similar posters for the LMS in 1924. Recently seven of his original railway poster paintings were found behind a wardrobe in a North London house and were given reserve prices of up to £9,500 each! Even his printed railway posters can fetch £2,000 each.

Terence Cuneo (1907-1996)

The doyen of post-war railway artists, Terence Cuneo studied at Chelsea Polytechnic and the Slade School of Art before going on to become a magazine and book illustrator. During World War II he worked as an artist for the *Illustrated London News* before being appointed as an official war artist, producing illustrations of aircraft factories and wartime events for the War Artists Advisory Committee and at the same time serving as a sapper. Following the end of the war Cuneo was commissioned to produce oil paintings of railway infrastructure and locomotives; Cuneo often took great risks when sketching on location, the highlight must have been being lashed to the top of the Forth Bridge during a gale! His big break came when he was appointed the official artist for the Coronation of Queen Elizabeth II in 1953. Following this he was in great demand not only as an industrial and military artist but also as a railway poster artist, producing some widely acclaimed works for the British Transport Commission and British Railways. 'Clapham Junction' (produced for the Southern Region) and the 'Centenary of the Royal Albert Bridge' (produced for the Western Region) are just two of his fine works depicting life on British Railways during the late steam period. He went on to tackle the diesel and electric era, every painting having his tiny mouse trademark hidden away in the most unlikely place.

In addition to his railway paintings he is also well known for his vast number of paintings commissioned by British Army regiments illustrating battles in

World War II, the Falklands War and the Gulf War. Original Cuneo paintings and even his British Railway's posters are much sought after – in recent years some of his original railway paintings have been fetching up to £50,000. His paintings have appeared on British postage stamps, an InterCity train was named after him in 1990 and a statue to him has recently been unveiled at Waterloo station.

DOLGOCH STATION
ON THE
TALYLLYN RAILWAY
TOWYN MERIONETH WALES

THE FIRST SEVERN BRIDGE
The story of the Severn railway bridge

For centuries the lowest crossing of the River Severn was at Gloucester and until the building of the Severn Railway Bridge further downstream trains between Bristol and South Wales were forced to take a long and circuitous route through the city.

Close to the Welsh border to the west of the River Severn lies the ancient Forest of Dean, an important source of iron ore and coal since medieval times. The opening of the then narrow gauge Severn & Wye Railway & Canal Company in 1813 linked the Severn at Lydney and the Wye at Lydbrook and provided an outlet for the output of these mines. In reality a horse-drawn tramway, this steeply-graded line was ripe for modernisation by the time the broad gauge South Wales Railway had opened along the west bank of the Severn in 1851. However, it took another 18 years before the Severn & Wye (S&W) was relaid to broad gauge and steam power was introduced. By then Brunel's broad gauge was in decline and the railway was converted to standard gauge in 1874.

On the opposite side of the Severn the Midland Railway's four-mile branch from Berkeley Road, on the Bristol to Gloucester main line, to docks at Sharpness opened in 1876. By then coal trains from the Forest of Dean to Bristol and the Southwest had to travel the long way round via Gloucester. Bridging the gap between the Severn & Wye Railway at Lydney and the Midland Railway at Sharpness seemed the obvious answer and thus was the Severn Bridge Railway born.

Authorised in 1872, the Severn Bridge Railway, financially backed by the S&W and the MR, involved the building of four miles of railway from Sharpness to Lydney via a 1,387yd-long bridge over the River Severn. The 22 cast-iron spans were 70ft above the river with one of them operating as a swing bridge where it crossed the Gloucester and Sharpness Canal. Work began in 1875 but the company soon faced financial problems and was jointly bought out by the GWR and the MR, becoming the Severn & Wye & Severn Bridge Joint Railway (S&W&SBJR). The bridge finally opened on 17 October 1879 but its usefulness soon disappeared when the Severn Tunnel was opened further downstream in 1886. Meanwhile the Severn & Wye Railway & Canal Company was also facing financial problems and in 1894 it merged with the S&W&SBJR to become the Severn & Wye Joint Railway, jointly owned by the GWR and MR.

Passenger services over the bridge consisted of six trains each way on weekdays, the majority taking just over 1½ hours for the 20½-mile journey between Berkeley Road and Lydbrook Junction. A new loop was opened in 1908 at Berkeley Road enabling freight trains from the bridge to travel south to Westerleigh, where there was a connection with the GWR's new Badminton cut-off line, and Bristol. This was also used as a diversionary route when the Severn Tunnel was closed, usually on a Sunday, for maintenance.

Passenger services north of Lydney ceased as early as 1929 from which date

Severn Bridge.

trains from Berkeley Road via the Severn Bridge terminated at Lydney Town. Hauled by GWR 0-6-0 pannier tanks, the pattern of six passenger trains each way continued into BR days and provided a link for schoolchildren who lived on one side of the Severn but went to school on the opposite side. The end abruptly came for the Severn Railway Bridge on a foggy 25 October 1960 when two loaded petroleum barges heading up river to Sharpness were swept into one of the support columns, causing two of the spans to collapse. Luckily no train was on the bridge but five people on the boats died in the accident.

Damaged in a further accident in 1961 the bridge was never repaired, leaving the remaining four-mile branch from Berkeley Road to Sharpness served by an auto train until closure on 31 October 1964. The bridge was later dismantled but the stone circular pier of the swing bridge at Sharpness can still be seen today and the foundations of some of the bridge's piers can be spotted in the mud at low tide. The Sharpness branch is still in situ having been used by scrap metal trains to Sharpness Docks and nuclear flask trains from Berkeley Power Station.

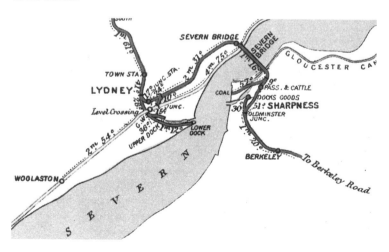

SMALL IS BEAUTIFUL
The story of two long-lost narrow gauge railways

SNAILBEACH DISTRICT RAILWAYS

Set in the shadow of the craggy Stiperstones Hills in Shropshire, the 2ft 4in (some sources say 2ft 3¾in) gauge Snailbeach District Railways was opened from Pontesbury (on the joint GWR/LNWR branch line from Shrewsbury to Minsterley) to lead mines at Snailbeach in 1877. With a total length of only 3¾ miles this curiously gauged line was initially profitable but the closure of the largest mine in 1884 led to a decline in the railway's fortunes – during this moribund time the Snailbeach's two locomotives were loaned to the expanding Glyn Valley Tramway in the Ceiriog Valley to the north.

The Snailbeach came back to life again in 1905 when a rail-linked granite quarry near Habberley was opened – to work this traffic the railway borrowed one of the Glyn Valley Tramway's 2ft 4½in gauge locos but soon returned it because of the slight difference in gauge, instead buying a Bagnall 0-6-0T 'Dennis'. Granite stone traffic remained buoyant for a few years but by 1915 this had dwindled considerably and the line closed.

Following the end of World War I granite for road building came back in demand and Shropshire County Council leased the granite quarry. Seeing another money-making venture beckoning, Colonel Holman Fred Stephens, owner of a ramshackle railway empire, bought the line and re-equipped it with two Baldwin 2-6-0 tanks that had previously worked in northern France during the war. The opening of a stone-crushing plant soon brought plenty of work for the railway and through the 1930s it prospered, carrying crushed granite to the exchange sidings at Pontesbury.

By 1947 the Snailbeach's steam locomotives were on their last legs and they were soon scrapped. Shropshire County Council leased what was left of the railway, sending loaded stone wagons by gravity downhill to Pontesbury and hauling them back to the quarry by a tractor straddling the line. This antiquated operation ceased in 1959 when the line from the quarry was converted into a road.

CAMPBELTOWN & MACHRIHANISH LIGHT RAILWAY

Once dubbed the 'Whisky Capital of the World' the harbour town of Campbeltown at the far south of the isolated Mull of Kintyre was also once home to an eccentric narrow gauge railway. Opened in 1877 to replace a disused canal, the 2ft 3in gauge 4½-mile Campbeltown & Machrihanish Light Railway served coal mines near Machrihanish.

The line initially flourished, carrying coal to the harbour at Campbeltown and was rebuilt and extended as a passenger-carrying light railway in 1906. Carried on fast turbine steamers from Glasgow, daytrippers were conveyed the 6½ miles from Argyll Street station in Campbeltown to the beaches and golf links at Machrihanish. With a break during World War I the railway continued to flourish through the 1920s but competition from road buses and the closure of the Argyll Colliery in 1929 soon brought about its demise. The line closed in November 1931, briefly reopening early in 1932 but closing for good in May of that year. Within a year the track had been lifted, the two 0-6-2 tank locomotives 'Atlantic' and 'Argyll' scrapped and the company wound up.

Nothing much remains of this unique Scottish narrow gauge line today although the scene in Argyll Street, Campbeltown, is much the same. The route of the railway alongside Campbeltown Loch and through a long cutting up to Limecraigs can easily be followed – the latter is now a footpath and cycleway. Elsewhere the trackbed has long since disappeared under ploughed fields but at Machrihanish the route of the railway can still be traced close to the site of the terminus behind the former Ugadale Arms Hotel.

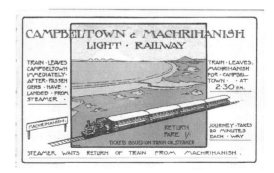

'THE SLOW, MISERABLE & JOLTY'
The story of the Stratford-upon-Avon & Midland Junction Railway

Once grandly titled 'The Shakespeare Route', the cross-country Stratford-upon-Avon & Midland Junction Railway (SMJR) was formed in 1909-10 by the amalgamation of four existing but bankrupt railways.

First on the scene was the Northampton & Banbury Junction Railway (N&BJR) which opened from Blisworth, on the LNWR main line, to Towcester in 1866 and from Towcester to Cockley Brake Junction, on the LNWR's branch from Verney Junction to Banbury, in 1872. Built to serve ironstone mines around Blisworth, the company briefly changed its name to the Midland Counties & South Wales Railway but a proposed lengthy extension to Ross-on-Wye in Gloucestershire was soon forgotten and the company reverted to its original name. Cheaper imported ironstone from Spain soon put an end to the railway's brief period of profitability.

The second of the SMJR's constituent railways was the East & West Junction Railway (E&WJR) which was authorised in 1864 to build a 38¼-mile line from Stratford-upon-Avon to Towcester. Following years of financial problems the line eventually opened in 1872 but it was continually beset by problems, being run by an Official Receiver for many years with its passenger service suspended.

Next on the scene was the Evesham, Redditch & Stratford-upon-Avon Railway which was authorised to build a 7¾-mile line from Broom Junction, on the Evesham & Redditch Railway, to Stratford-upon-Avon where it would meet the aforementioned E&WJR. It opened in 1879 but was also soon in trouble, with an Official Receiver being appointed in 1886.

The final SMJR constituent company was the Stratford-upon-Avon, Towcester & Midland Junction Railway which was authorised to build a line from Ravenstone Wood Junction, on the Midland Railway's Bedford to Northampton branch, to Towcester, crossing above the LNWR's main line at Roade. Opened in 1891 it, too, was soon in financial trouble and passenger services were hurriedly withdrawn with an Official Receiver being appointed in 1898.

Despite together offering an east-west cross-country route with numerous mainline connections, these four motley and financially bankrupt railways were in dire straits by the end of the 19th century. None of the major neighbouring railway companies were interested in purchasing them so the SMJR was formed by the amalgamation of three of these companies in 1909. The fourth, the N&BJR, joined in 1910.

The opening of the Great Central Railway's London Extension in 1899, with a connecting spur to the E&WJR at Woodford & Hinton (later Woodford Halse), saw through carriages running between Marylebone and Stratford-upon-Avon, hence its marketing name as 'The Shakespeare Route'. The SMJR also became an important through route for Midland Railway freight traffic between Bristol and St Pancras, via Ashchurch and Broom Junction. Local passenger traffic was sparse with three return journeys between Blisworth and Stratford sufficing on weekdays and its worn out and decrepit track soon earned the railway the nickname of the 'Slow, Miserable and Jolty'!

The SMJR became part of the LMS in 1923 and not only grew as an important east-west route for freight traffic bypassing Birmingham but also for excursion traffic until World War II. A Karrier Ro-Railer converted single-decker bus was also tried out by the LMS but this service

was unsuccessful and was withdrawn after a short time in 1932. Following the war, passenger services were withdrawn between Broom Junction and Stratford in 1947 and between Blisworth and Stratford in 1952. Blisworth to Cockley Brake closed completely in 1951 and Blisworth to Ravenstone Junction similarly in 1952. Now under the control of the Western Region of British Railways, freight continued to use the SMJR for some more years, including a growing number of iron ore trains (usually hauled by '9F' 2-10-0s or 'WD' 2-8-0s) from Northamptonshire to South Wales which ran via a new connection with the Honeybourne line at Stratford which had opened in 1960. From that date the section west to Broom Junction closed completely. By 1965 the ironstone traffic to South Wales had declined and the remaining SMJR route was closed completely on 5 July with the exception of the section from Fenny Compton that still serves the MOD depot near Kineton.

FOOTNOTE: The author well remembers a lengthy railtour organised by the Gloucestershire Railway Society in 1961 which travelled to Derby Works via Ashchurch, Evesham, Redditch and Birmingham then back on a lengthy and convoluted journey to Blisworth where it joined the SMJR route to Stratford-upon-Avon. The engine, a preserved MR Compound 4-4-0 No. 1000, stalled on the climb out of Blisworth, coming to a complete halt until copious amounts of sand had been sprinkled on the rails and progress very slowly resumed. Happy days!

STOP PRESS
Railway news, December 1929

A vine at Knebworth LNER station has this season yielded 80 bunches of fine Black Homburg grapes. The vine is 30 years old and grows along the glass roof of a subway within a few feet of the track over which the 'Flying Scotsman' passes at 60 miles an hour every day.

The LNER have recently introduced a new all-electric cooking and refrigerating kitchen and restaurant car on the 8.15pm 'Hook Continental' from Liverpool Street. This is the first electric restaurant car to be run on a Continental Boat Express.

On Friday, November 1st, 'The Southern Belle', the famous all-Pullman train that runs between London (Victoria) and Brighton, celebrated its 21st anniversary. The occasion was observed with befitting festivity. The departure platform at Victoria was gaily decorated with flags and the engine – 'Sir Ontzlake' of the 'King Arthur' type – that drew the train, also was dressed up. In spite of some fog in the neighbourhood of London the run to Brighton was made in 59 minutes, one minute under schedule time.

During these winter months the up 'Cheltenham Flyer' is well maintaining the high standard of running demanded by its stiff schedule of 77¼ miles (Swindon to Paddington) in 70 minutes. On a Saturday in November when there were two coaches beyond the normal load, the engine No. 4089 'Donnington Castle' made the run in 70mins 33secs notwithstanding two severe checks at Didcot and between Burnham Beeches and Slough. Such times show that even the lightning schedules now in vogue have no terrors for modern GWR locomotives.

WAR SERVICE
Foreign service for Britain's railways in World War I

The Railway Operating Division (ROD) of the Royal Engineers was formed in 1915 to operate both standard gauge and narrow gauge railways in theatres of conflict during World War I.

War Department Light Railways
By 1915 both sides in the bloody 'Great War' had ground to a halt, digging in with a trench system that stretched from the English Channel to the Swiss border. Supplying the front line from the nearest standard gauge railhead was fraught with difficulties with early lorries proving useless in the mud-soaked and shell-blasted landscape. Horses, used in their hundreds of thousands, were the only answer for pulling artillery, ambulances and supply wagons. However, at the beginning of the war they were in short supply and nearly a million had to be brought from overseas for service with the British Army.

Prior to the war both the Germans and French had developed lightweight 60cm gauge light railways that could quickly be laid and provide a flow of equipment and stores to the front line. On the British side the Royal Engineers had decided in their wisdom that motor lorries would be more effective – how wrong they were and it wasn't until 1916 that the Minister of Munitions recommended the use of tactical light railways.

By 1917 the War Department Light Railways were using narrow gauge 4-6-0 tank locomotives, supplied mainly by Hunslet, Kerr Stuart, ALCO and the US company Baldwin. These were successfully used in rear areas moving supplies from standard gauge railheads to marshalling yards nearer the front. From here supplies were moved to the front line by small and unobtrusive 0-4-0 petrol tractors mainly supplied by the Motor Rail & Tramcar Company – around 1,000 Simplex tractors, some of them armoured, saw active service during the war.

Following the end of the war some Baldwin 4-6-0 tank locomotives saw service on four British narrow gauge railways – Ashover Light Railway, Glyn Valley Tramway, Welsh Highland Railway and Snailbeach District Railway. An example that once served in India has been preserved on the Leighton Buzzard Narrow Gauge Railway.

Railway Operating Division of the Royal Engineers (ROD)

As the two opposing sides in the war ground to a bloody halt the French standard gauge railway system became increasingly incapable of handling the vast amounts of ammunition and supplies needed to sustain the Allied front line. By 1916 the ROD had already started to requisition locomotives and rolling stock from British railway companies for use, not only in France, but also further afield in Mesopotamia, Greece, Palestine, the Balkans and Italy. Around 600 locos (mainly 0-6-0 goods locos) and thousands of wagons were sent abroad from the South Eastern & Chatham Railway, London, Brighton & South Coast Railway, London & South Western Railway, Great Western Railway, London & North Western Railway, Midland Railway, Lancashire &

Yorkshire Railway, Caledonian Railway, North Eastern Railway, Great Central Railway, Great Northern Railway, Great Eastern Railway and North British Railway. It must have been a strange sight for soldiers seeing GWR 'Deans Goods' or 'Moguls' working freight trains in northern France. Despite a few being lost at sea most of these locos survived the war and were either sold to the host nation or returned home.

As the war dragged on the demand for heavy freight locos outstripped supply so the ROD adopted the Great Central Railway's Class '8K' 2-8-0 as its standard freight locomotive. Designed by John Robinson the 521 locos were built in various batches by the GCR, North British Locomotive Company, Robert Stephenson and Nasmyth Wilson and Kitson.

These powerful freight locos were so successful that when they returned home after the war many were bought by the GWR (100), LNER (273) and LMS (105). A few even went to Australia where three of them have since been preserved.

Many of the ROD 2-8-0s were called up again during World War II, seeing active service in Egypt, Palestine, Syria and Iraq. Many British examples survived into the BR era with the last being withdrawn in 1966. Only one, No. 63601, has survived.

GWR FAMOUS TRAINS
The Bristolian

'The Bristolian' express was introduced in 1935 to mark the Centenary of the GWR. Travelling non-stop between Paddington and Bristol the lightweight train of only seven carriages was initially hauled by 'King' Class 4-6-0s and was timed to take 1hr 45min for the outward journey of 118¼ miles via Bath and for the return journey of 117½ miles via the Badminton cut-off. Before World War II, when the train was temporarily suspended, the up 'The Bristolian' left Paddington at 10am and the down train left Bristol at 4.30pm.

The service was reinstated in 1954 with an 8.45am departure from Paddington and a 4.30pm return from Bristol, thus giving businessmen more time for their meetings in Bristol. Still normally 'King'-hauled the timings were identical to pre-war days but the modification of some 'Castle' Class 4-6-0 locos soon brought some electrifying performances.

Built in 1949, 'Castle' Class No. 7018 'Drysllwyn Castle' was the first of its class to be fitted with a double chimney and four-row superheater. Emerging

from Swindon Works with its modifications in May 1956, the Bristol (Bath Road)-allocated loco was soon putting up electrifying 100mph performances on the 'The Bristolian'. Soon other 'Castles' were similarly modified and the train occasionally completed the up journey via Badminton in under 94 minutes at an average speed of 75mph. The sound of the 4-cylinder beat of a 'Castle' as it roared through Swindon at 80mph was a thrilling experience for any young lad, the author included! The introduction of Swindon-built 'Warship' Class diesels in 1959 soon put an end to this steam spectacular – the last up steam-hauled train being hauled by No. 5085 'Evesham Abbey' on 12 June.

The 'Warship' and later 'Western' Class diesel hydraulics were replaced by HST 125s in 1976 and what purported to be 'The Bristolian' became just another anonymous train.

Flash forward to 2010 when restored Castle' Class 4-6-0 No. 5043 'Earl of Mount Edgcumbe' hauled a commemorative 'The Bristolian' to mark the 175th Anniversary of the GWR. Its return journey from Bristol to Paddington was completed in just under 1hr 50min, only five minutes slower than the 1950s schedule, arriving at its destination 45 minutes early – Messrs Churchward and Collett must have had smiles on their faces when looking down from GWR Heaven!

Cambrian Coast Express

The first through trains between Paddington and Aberystwyth began on 14 July 1921 when a Luncheon and Tea Car Express was introduced by the GWR and Cambrian Railways. Leaving London at 10.15am the train changed engines on the Shrewsbury avoiding line where two Cambrian Railways 4-4-0s would take over for the rest of the journey to Aberystwyth, arriving at 4.20pm. Through carriages were also conveyed for Pwllheli, arriving at 5.45pm.

This train became officially known as the 'Cambrian Coast Express' in 1927 by which time the Cambrian Railways had become part of the GWR. Initially only running during the summer, the train ran officially 'non-stop' between Wolverhampton (Low Level) and Welshpool but actually stopped on the

Shrewsbury avoiding line where two GWR 'Dukedog' 4-4-0s would take over for the rest of the journey. New 'Manor' Class 4-6-0s were introduced for this last leg of the journey after World War II and these continued in service until 1965 when BR Standard Class 4 4-6-0s took over until 1967. By then the 'Castle' Class 4-6-0s had already been replaced for the Paddington to Shrewsbury leg of the journey by Brush Type 4 diesels with the train changing engines at Shrewsbury station.

Following World War II the 'CCE'

11 Cambrian Coast Express

WEEKDAYS

		E a.m.	S a.m.
London (Paddington)	dep.	10A10	10A50
			p.m.
Banbury General	arr.	11 20	12 11
	dep.	11 22	12 15
Leamington Spa	arr.	—	12 39
General	dep.	—	12 43
		p.m.	
Birmingham (Snow Hill)	arr.	12 13	1 15
	dep.	12 17	1 20
Wolverhampton (Low Level)	arr.	12 37	1 39
	dep.	12 44	1 46
Shrewsbury	arr.	1 19	—
	dep.	1 23	—
Welshpool	arr.	2 1	2 56
Newtown	,,	2 30	3 28
Machynlleth	,,	3 20	4 18
Machynlleth	dep.	3 40	4 30
Penhelig Halt	arr.	4 2	—
Aberdovey	,,	4 6	4 51
Towyn	,,	4 14	5 2
Tonfanau	,,	4 21	—
Llwyngwril	,,	4 32	5 15
Fairbourne	,,	4 40	5 24
Barmouth Junction	,,	4 44	5 27
Barmouth	,,	4 50	5 33
Harlech	,,	5 17	6 0
Portmadoc	,,	5 38	6 21
Criccieth	,,	5 50	6 35
Pwllheli	,,	6 10	7 0
Machynlleth	dep.	3 25	4 23
Borth	arr.	3 45	4 46
Aberystwyth	,,	4 5	5 10

		S a.m.	E a.m.
Aberystwyth	dep.	9A25	11A45
Borth	,,	9A45	12A 5
Dovey Junction	arr.	10 0	12 25
Pwllheli	dep.	—	9A55
Criccieth	,,	—	10A14
Portmadoc	,,	—	10A25
Harlech	,,	—	10A50
Barmouth	,,	—	11A20
Barmouth Junction	,,	8A45	11A26
Fairbourne	,,	8A50	11A29
Llwyngwril	,,	9A 5	11A40
Tonfanau	,,	9 15	11 48
Towyn	,,	9A22	11A59
Aberdovey	,,	9A30	12A 6
Penhelig Halt	,,	9 36	12 10
Dovey Junction	arr.	9 50	12 23
			p.m.
Dovey Junction	dep.	10A 8	12A33
Machynlleth	,,	10A20	12A43
Newtown	,,	11 17	1 35
Welshpool	,,	11 55	2 7
Shrewsbury	arr.	—	2 42
	dep.	—	2 52
		p.m.	
Wolverhampton (Low Level)	arr.	1 11	3 30
	dep.	1 18	3 35
Birmingham (Snow Hill)	arr.	1 38	3 55
	dep.	1 42	4 0
Leamington Spa	arr.	2 11	4 23
General	dep.	2 13	4 25
London (Paddington)	arr.	4 10	6 0

A—Seats can be reserved in advance on payment of a fee of 2s. 0d. per seat.

E—Except Saturdays.

S—Saturdays only.

RESTAURANT CAR SERVICE available between Paddington and Aberystwyth in each direction.

was a Summer-Saturdays only train until 1959 when it started operating on weekdays all year round. Regional boundary changes soon saw it transferred from Paddington to Euston and, following the end of steam on the Cambrian section in 1967, this final leg of the journey was taken over by BR Sulzer Type 2 diesels. The last train ran in 1991.

RESERVOIR DOGS
The story of two corporation-owned water works railways

Towards the end of the 19th century the need for dependable and clean water supplies for the growing industrialised cities of Britain led several city corporations to look further afield. The building of reservoirs by damming remote rural valleys was a triumph of Victorian engineering which has stood the test of time. The construction of these dams, reservoirs and aqueducts required vast amounts of raw material and construction workers. The sites of the reservoirs were often in remote regions that had poor roads so the building of a railway to carry workers and construction materials was the only answer. Here is the story of two of these railways.

The Elan Valley Railway
Owned and operated by the Birmingham Corporation Water Department, the standard gauge Elan Valley Railway was opened in 1896. From a junction

with the Cambrian Railways' Mid-Wales line just south of Rhayader the 'main line' extended for nine miles up the remote Elan Valley to the site of the furthest dam at Craig Coch. At its maximum extent, including branch lines and sidings, the railway extended to 33 miles, serving construction sites for dams at Craig Coch, Penygarreg, Carreg-ddu and Caban-coch reservoirs. The single-track line, with gradients as steep as 1 in 33, also served Elan village, where navvies lived in an alcohol-free shanty town and had exchange sidings with the Cambrian Railways at Neuadd. From here the Elan Valley Railway's own locomotives, built by Manning Wardle and Hunslet and named after the streams that fed the reservoirs, worked the goods, workmen's and schoolchildren's trains. The Elan Valley reservoirs were linked to Birmingham via a 73-mile aqueduct; its gradient of 1 in 2,300 meant that water took 36 hours to reach Frankley reservoir on the outskirts of the city and the building of the dams and the subsequent flooding of the Elan Valley had several side effects, including the submergence of farms but principally the loss of the former home of the Victorian romantic poet, Percy Shelley.

By 1904 the reservoirs were nearing completion and the Elan Valley Railway was preparing for a right royal visit. On 21 July the royal train, carrying King Edward VII and Queen Alexandra, which had travelled from Swansea via the Central Wales line and the connecting spur at Builth Road, reached Rhayader station. From here the royal visitors were carried in ancient four-wheeled Cambrian Railways' coaches headed by Manning Wardle 0-6-0T 'Calettwr' for an inspection of what was then still a giant building site. Despite the royal visit construction of the dams and reservoirs was not completed until 1906 by which time the Elan Valley Railway had served its purpose. The branch lines to the various dams had been closed by 1912 and the 'main line' to Craig Coch was closed in 1916.

Despite the long passage of time since closure, much of the route of the Elan Valley Railway can be followed today. Known as the Elan Valley Trail, an eight-mile footpath and cycleway from Cwmdauddwr (south of Rhayader) to Craig Goch dam follows the route of the old railway line around four of the

Elan Valley reservoirs and their dams. A visitor centre has been converted from the old railway workshops and the adjacent car park was once the site of the locomotive shed and sidings.

The Nidd Valley Light Railway

With its thriving textile industry the 'boom town' and the 'wool capital of the world' of Bradford was at bursting point by the last decade of the 19th century. At the turn of the 19th century Bradford was a small market town with a population of 16,000; by 1850 this had reached 182,000 and by 1891 it was over 200,000 souls. Clean drinking water was in short supply, a situation that created ideal conditions for cholera and typhoid, leading to an average life expectancy of just under 19 years.

Looking further afield for a supply of clean water Bradford Corporation's Water Works Committee built a reservoir in the Nidd Valley at Gouthwaite, 40 miles to the north of the city between Pateley Bridge and Ramsgill. An aqueduct and underground pipeline linked Gouthwaite Reservoir to Chellow Heights Reservoir on the outskirts of Bradford. Unlike the Elan Valley scheme no large-scale railway was built to serve the site as most of the raw materials needed for building the dam were obtained locally.

By the end of the century the people of Nidderdale were clamouring for their own railway. A 14-mile branch line had already been opened by the North Eastern Railway in 1862 from Harrogate to Pateley Bridge. Authorised in 1901 as a narrow gauge railway, the Nidd Valley Light Railway opened for traffic as a standard gauge line between Pateley Bidge and Lofthouse-in-Nidderdale in 1907. Even before the line was built it had been taken over by Bradford Corporation Waterworks Committee who had plans to build two further reservoirs in the Nidd Valley. There was, however, one problem and that was that the Light Railway Order stipulated that a passenger service also had to be run over the line as far as Lofthouse – in buying the line Bradford Corporation became the first local authority in the country to own a public railway. Another problem was that the Nidd Valley terminus at Pateley Bridge was a quarter of a mile away from the NER terminus – passengers who had arrived by NER train were often perplexed by the total lack of signage and Nidderdale's brave new  integrated transport system often failed at the first hurdle!

The two new reservoirs at Angram and Scar House were completed in 1904 and 1921 respectively. Beyond Lofthouse there was a further six miles of goods-only line to Scar House and Angram Reservoirs, so steeply graded that even short goods trains often required four locomotives (two at the front and two at the rear). Workmen's trains also travelled along this route serving the navvies' temporary villages (complete with hospital, school, mission hall, bank and social hall) built at the dam construction sites. The passenger service consisted of four return trains each weekday but this was reduced to three each way in 1918 and in order to reduce running costs a second-hand steam railcar was bought from the Great Western Railway in 1920. Soon, competition from road transport up the valley was having a negative effect on the railway's finances and closure to passengers came on 31 December 1929.

Despite the loss of passenger services the line lived on until the completion of Scar House Reservoir in September 1936. After this the fate of the railway was sealed and it was all sold, lock, stock and barrel, in a mega auction in June 1937.

Today while station buildings at Pateley Bridge, Wath, Ramsgill and Lofthouse still survive – albeit with different uses – much of the trackbed between Pateley Bridge and Gouthwaite Reservoir is a footpath. A display about the railway can be seen in the Nidderdale Museum in Pateley Bridge.

TRAM LINES
The Light Railway Transport League

By the 1930s the writing was on the wall for Britain's electric street tramways and by the outbreak of World War II the majority had been closed and replaced by electric trolley buses or diesel buses. The last electric trams in South London, operating out of New Cross depot, were withdrawn in 1952. Electric street trams clung on to life for a few more years in other cities – Birmingham and Sunderland until 1954, Dundee and Edinburgh until 1956, Liverpool until 1957, Aberdeen until 1958, Leeds until 1959, Sheffield and Swansea & Mumbles until 1960 and those in Glasgow until 1962.

In more recent years electric street trams have seen a renaissance in Britain, and there are now systems operating (most having a mixture of on-street running and reserved track) in Sheffield, Manchester, Croydon and Nottingham. A tramway system in Edinburgh is currently under construction albeit held up by many delays and there are also proposals for similar systems in Bristol, Leeds and Liverpool.

But back in the dark days of the 1930s a group of modern tramway supporters, headed by Jay Fowler, got together to form the Light Railway Transport League. It was officially established on 30 June 1937 and was soon publishing a monthly magazine, *The Modern Tramway*. The League also went on to organise tours of surviving tramway systems with their first, in 1938, taking in a 60-mile tour of the London tramway system. So successful was this that others were soon being organised around Britain

LIGHT RAILWAY
TRANSPORT LEAGUE.

21st
Anniversary
Celebration

Held at the
WINDSOR HOTEL,
Lancaster Gate, W.2,
on SATURDAY, 22nd NOVEMBER, 1958,

CHACKLEY T. HUMPEDGE, B.Sc.(C.Eng.), M.Inst.T.
PRESIDENT.

and even to Holland and Belgium. Even the onset of World War II didn't deter the members who continued to publish their magazine and even held a meeting in an air-raid shelter!

Another magazine, *Tramway Review,* was introduced in 1950. Still in publication, this quarterly publication devotes itself to historical material while *The Modern Tramway* (now superceded by *Tramways & Urban Transport*) was about modern news and developments. The League changed its name to the Light Rail Transit Association in 1979 and soon found its beliefs in such systems to be vindicated with the opening of the Tyne & Wear Metro, the Docklands Light Railway and the Manchester and Sheffield tramway systems.

Menu.

Cream of Tomato Soup
or Hors-d'oeuvre.

Roast Surrey Chicken
and York Ham.
Creamed and Roast Potatoes.
Garden Peas.

Apricot Flan.
Ice Cream.

Coffee.

Toasts.

The Queen.
The President.

The Light Railway Transport League.
Sir Patrick Dollan, D.L., LL.D., J.P.
Reply by J. W. Fowler, A.M.Inst.B.E., Chairman of Council.

The Passenger Transport Industry.
Major C. S. N. Walker, J.P.
Reply by Chaceley T. Humpidge, B.Sc.(C.Eng.),
M.Inst.T., President of League.

Modern European Tramways.
R. K. Kirkland, B.A., A.K.C.
Reply by G. A. Meier, A.M.I.E.E.,
Chief Engineer, Zurich Tramways, Vice-President.

The Guests and Ladies.
G. B. Claydon, LL.B., Area Representative, Birmingham.
Reply by C. F. Klapper, M.Inst.T.
and Mrs. B. Jackson.

HAPPY BIRTHDAY, GWR
Celebrating the centenary of the Great Western Railway

1 935 was an important year for the Great Western Railway as it was exactly 100 years since the company had received its enabling Act of Parliament to build a railway between London and Bristol. Engineered by Isambard Kingdom Brunel, the railway transformed communications between the two cities, providing what was then a fast and comfortable service unheard of in the days of the stage coach.

Over the next 100 years the GWR spread its tentacles to nearly every part of the South-West, South, west and mid-Wales and the Midlands. Divesting itself of Brunel's broad gauge by 1892 the company had gone on to build world-beating steam locomotives at Swindon under the regimes of successive brilliant chief mechanical engineers –William Dean, George Jackson Churchward and Charles Collet. Joined by almost 50 more companies in the 'Big Four' Grouping of 1923 the company by then owned nearly 4,000 route miles of railway, operated a fleet of ships, numerous commercial docks and a chain of luxury hotels and had pioneered road motor transport and airline services. By 1935 the company had become a household name and along with its loyal workforce well deserved its title of 'God's Wonderful Railway'!

The GWR chose to celebrate

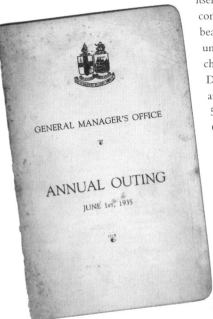

GENERAL MANAGER'S OFFICE

ANNUAL OUTING

JUNE 1st, 1935

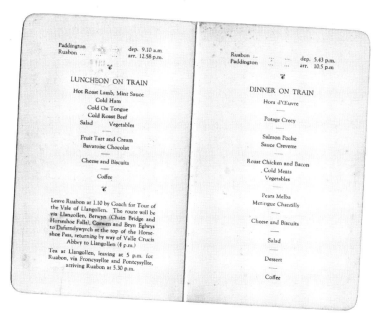

Paddington ... ... dep. 9.10 a.m
Ruabon ... ... arr. 12.58 p.m.

LUNCHEON ON TRAIN

Hot Roast Lamb, Mint Sauce
Cold Ham
Cold Ox Tongue
Cold Roast Beef
Salad   Vegetables

Fruit Tart and Cream
Bavaroise Chocolat

Cheese and Biscuits

Coffee

Leave Ruabon at 1.10 by Coach for Tour of
the Vale of Llangollen. The route will be
via Llangollen, Berwyn (Chain Bridge and
Horseshoe Falls), Corwen and Bryn Eglwys
to Dafarndywyrch at the top of the Horseshoe Pass, returning by way of Valle Crucis
Abbey to Llangollen (4 p.m.)

Tea at Llangollen, leaving at 5 p.m. for
Ruabon, via Froncysyllte and Pontcysyllte,
arriving Ruabon at 5.30 p.m.

Ruabon ... ... dep. 5.43 p.m.
Paddington ... ... arr. 10.5 p.m

DINNER ON TRAIN

Hors d'Œuvre

Potage Crecy

Salmon Poche
Sauce Crevette

Roast Chicken and Bacon
Cold Meats
Vegetables

Pears Melba
Meringue Chantilly

Cheese and Biscuits

Salad

Dessert

Coffee

its centenary in a grand fashion, befitting the status of the company, but more
about this later. However, before the actual day arrived, many departments of
the GWR set about organising special events for their staff.

The General Manager of the GWR Hotels department organised a cracker
for his staff on 1 June. His Annual Outing consisted of a special train leaving
Paddington at 9.10am and arriving at Ruabon a 12.58pm. En route the party
were served luncheon while at Ruabon they detrained for a coach tour of the
Vale of Llangollen, visiting Chain Bridge, Horseshoe Falls, Horseshoe Pass and
Valle Crucis Abbey. On their return they stopped at Llangollen for tea before
boarding their train at Ruabon for the return journey to Paddington. After
departing at 5.43pm the party was served a splendid dinner before arriving
back in London at 10.5pm.

LIST OF GUESTS

A.	Table Number.
W. H. Ackland, Esq.	20
A. F. Adams, Esq.	26
G. G. Adams, Esq.	24
H. C. Adams, Esq.	10
Rowland Adams, Esq.	26
W. J. Adams, Esq.	34
M. E. Adcock, Esq.	25
W. A. D. Alexander, Esq.	10
A. S. Allen, Esq.	33
C. J. Allen, Esq.	38
Sidney Allen, Esq.	1
E. W. Andrews, Esq.	24
The Lord Apsley.	1
Major The Hon. J. J. Astor.	1
J. Auld, Esq.	3
B.	
D.R.M. Baker	7
Humphrey Baker, Esq.	38
R. W. Baker, Esq.	4
L. Baldwin, Esq.	43
H. R. W. Bamberger, Esq.	29
W. J. Banks, Esq.	44
R. G. J. Barefoot, Esq.	29
H. V. Barnard, Esq.	10
Sir Percy E. Bates, Bt.	1
The Most Hon. The Marquess of Bath.	1
C. G. T. Bennett, Esq.	24
J. Bennett, Esq.	13
J. H. Bennett, Esq.	44
J. S. Bennett, Esq.	35 *24*
R. Bernays, Esq.	1
A. W. Betty, Esq.	25
J. F. Bicker, Esq.	24
J. F. Bickerton, Esq.	13
C. P. Billing Esq.	20
D. Blee, Esq.	12
W. Blenkin, Esq.	42
J. A. Bobbett, Esq.	32
Col. J. A. M. Bond.	17
G. H. Boucher., Esq.	29
H. G. Bowles, Esq.	12
T. A. Boxwell, Esq.	32 *11*
T. P. Bright, Esq.	21
R. Brodie, Esq.	43
John Bromley, Esq.	10
A. V. R. Brown, Esq.	41
W. Bryant, Esq.	24
C. T. Budgett, Esq.	20
J. H. Budgett, Esq.	10
Col. Dan Burges.	7
A. W. S. Burgess, Esq.	20
F. C. Burgess, Esq.	29
P. Burn, Esq.	41
F. M. Burris, Esq.	29
P. C. Burton, Esq.	17
E. S. Bush, Esq.	24
R. E. Bush, Esq.	21
Eric W. Butler, Esq.	29
Dr. T. Howard Butler.	29
W. H. Byrt, Esq.	24
C.	
~~Major E. Cadbury.~~	~~7~~
Sir John Cadman.	1
Hon. E. C. G. Cadogan.	7
P. W. Cann, Esq.	22
R. Carpmael, Esq.	16
Capt. E. Castle.	44

	Table Number.
H. E. Chattock, Esq.	29
R. F. Church, Esq.	39
S. R. Clabon, Esq.	25
W. E. Clapton, Esq.	41
C. Cyril Clarke, Esq.	10
Major F. L. Stanley Clarke.	6
R. S. W. Clarke, Esq.	9
F. F. Clothier, Esq.	20
A. J. Cole, Esq.	32
W. B. Cole, Esq.	44
C. B. Collett, Esq.	8
Sir Ernest H. Cook.	8
B. W. C. Cooke, Esq.	39
A. C. Cookson, Esq.	11 *4*
R. Cope, Esq.	8
G. Cornish, Esq.	33
S. W. Cornwell, Esq.	2
A. V. Cotterell, Esq.	35
F. C. A. Coventry, Esq.	15
F. N. Cowlin, Esq.	8
C. T. Cox, Esq.	26
S. Cox, Esq.	20
T. B. Cox, Esq.	44
E. T. Cozens, Esq.	22
W. Creighton, Esq.	21
F. S. Creswell, Esq.	21
P. E. Culverhouse, Esq.	27
R. G. Cunningham, Esq.	22
A. Curthoys, Esq.	40
J. O. Curtis, Esq.	32
D.	
Representative of " Daily Express."	38
Representative of " Daily Telegraph."	39
Col. S. H. G. Dainton.	8
C. R. Dashwood, Esq.	5
J. S. Davenport, Esq.	35
Miss Kathleen Howell Davies.	7
T. H. Davies, Esq.	1
F. R. E. Davis, Esq.	9
J. A. Denney, Esq.	44
M. J. M. Dewar, Esq.	38
A. Dowling, Esq.	19
~~A. H. Downes-Shaw, Esq.~~	~~22~~
The Right Hon. Lord Dulverton.	1
J. W. Duncan, Esq.	19
The Hon. J. M. Dunningham.	1
Major N. S. M. Durnford.	44
H. J. Dury, Esq.	35
E. M. Dyer, Esq.	18
E.	
Ellison F. Eberle, Esq.	9
~~J. F. Eberle, Esq.~~	~~19~~
~~V. Fuller Eberle, Esq.~~	~~9~~
A. E. Elliott, Esq.	35
Representative of " The Engineer."	39
~~F. England, Esq.~~	~~34~~
Henley S. Evans, Esq.	9
W. H. Eyles, Esq.	34
F.	
A. G. Farmer, Esq.	22
A. Follows, Esq.	35
Conrad Ford, Esq.	32
Eustace Ford, Esq.	32

	Table Number.
J. S. Frith, Esq.	35
W. D. Fripp, Esq.	9
Claude B. Fry, Esq.	20
H. H. Cavendish Fuller, Esq.	2
G.	
E. S. Gange, Esq.	30
G. E. Gedye, Esq.	35
M. F. Gibbons, Esq.	35
W. O. Gibbs, Esq.	21
C. R. Gill, Esq.	22
~~The Right Hon. Lord~~ *Glanely.*	~~34~~ *7*
John Gordon, Esq.	38
A. G. Gosling, Esq.	35
K. W. C. Grand, Esq.	39
John Green, Esq.	2 *19*
Josiah Green, Esq.	7
H. W. Griffin, Esq.	43
H. C. Griffith, Esq.	40
H. R. Griffiths, Esq.	11
H.	
F.C. Hall	33
A. Hadley, Esq.	43
F. M. Hall, Esq.	23
R. Halliday, Esq.	11
S. E. Halliwell, Esq.	43
C. J. Hambro, Esq.	1
Frank Harding, Esq.	34
W. R. Harford, Esq.	32
W. H. Harris, Esq.	36
E. Harvey, Esq.	33
J. St. C. Harvey, Esq.	9
C. Hathway, Esq.	42
H. W. Hawkins, Esq.	41
F. W. Hawksworth, Esq.	25
G. A. V. Hayes, Esq.	12
H. C. Hayes, Esq.	13
A. G. Heard, Esq.	23
H. E. Hedges, Esq.	12
G. H. Hedley, Esq.	33
G. T. Heming, Esq.	27
William Hewson, Esq.	43
J. H. Hickson, Esq.	39
V. A. Hillman, Esq.	16
F. A. Hoare, Esq.	22
A. H. Hobbs, Esq.	36
F. C. Hockridge, Esq.	14
C. Hartly Hodder, Esq.	1
W. Holloway, Esq.	44
Joseph Holman, Esq.	28
E. Hopkinson, Esq.	2
The Right Hon. Sir Robert Horne.	1
~~H. Hosegood, Esq.~~	~~16~~
A. G. Hubbard, Esq.	6
S. C. Humphries, Esq.	23
Sir Sidney R. W. Humphries.	7
Edward Hungerford, Esq.	17
C. G. Hutchings, Esq.	23
I.	
A. H. Ivey, Esq.	37
J.	
Sir Henry Mather Jackson, Bt.	1
C. M. Jacobs, Esq.	13
F. Jerrim, Esq.	28
H. John, Esq.	34
H. Jones, Esq.	16
J. E. Jones, Esq.	19

The list of guests at the GWR's centenary luncheon in Bristol on 31 August 1935.

	Table Number.
	14
q.	4
q.	44
	11
	40
	25
	39
sq.	30
	10
	41
	23
	42
d.	30
	31
	27
q.	1
	27
q.	1
	31
	6
	31
a.	39
	16
sq.	44
Esq.	2 9 *Powell*
Esq., M.P.	1
	6
	①
	1
	31
	34
n.	4
	37
sq.	34
sq.	14
	18
ng.	31
q.	37
a. Lord	1
lete.	1
	18
	31
	18
Esq.	27
"Morning	38
Mount.	17
q.	42
.	40
R. Sollon S. Esq.	16
sq.	14
sq.	2
"News	
	42
sq.	13
	3
	7
	40
, Esq.	19

P.

	Table Number.
H. A. Page, Esq.	2
~~C. S. Page, Esq.~~	~~4~~
The Right Hon. Lord Palmer.	1
F. Palmer, Esq.	4
H. Parkinson, Esq.	~~12~~ 2
O. J. Parry, Esq.	25
T. Paull, Esq.	25
W. F. Paull, Esq.	26
H. W. Payne, Esq.	32
J. L. Pearce, Esq.	28
W. N. Pellow, Esq.	20
W. G. Pelmear, Esq.	36
G. E. R. Penney, Esq.	12
Mrs. L. M. Pheysey.	8
D. Rupert Phillips, Esq.	16
G. H. Phillips, Esq.	36
P. W. Pine, Esq.	31
Col. R. B. Pitt.	7
W. A. Pitt, Esq.	3
W. J. Plogsted, Esq.	13
G. T. Plum, Esq.	3
R. G. Pole, Esq.	28
Major A. N. Pope.	16
S. C. Pope, Esq.	3
The Right Hon. Lord Portal.	1
F. R. Potter, Esq.	17
A. C. Powell, Esq.	16
Representative of " Press Association."	40

Q.

	Table Number.
A. S. Quartermaine, Esq.	19

R.

	Table Number.
C. H. Reed, Esq.	38
Representative of " Reynolds' Illustrated News."	42
G. W. Richards, Esq.	43
G. S. Rider, Esq.	11
G. I. Righton, Esq.	3
Sir Henry B. Robertson.	6
A. E. Robinson, Esq.	37
Foster G. Robinson, Esq.	8
P. G. Robinson, Esq.	2
W. Heath Robinson, Esq.	17
G. P. V. Rogers, Esq.	5
J. E. Rogers, Esq.	21
T. P. Rogers, Esq.	1
G. Rollason, Esq.	25
J. C. Rome, Esq.	26
S. G. Rowe, Esq.	21
H. J. G. Rudman, Esq.	30

S.

	Table Number.
R. Sollen, S. Esq.	16
J. E. Salter, Esq.	6
F. E. Sampson, Esq.	3
W. H. Sandell, Esq.	28
H. Sanders, Esq.	40
J. Scholar, Esq.	37
S. C. Seward, Esq.	21
C. E. Shackle, Esq.	13
G. Shallard, Esq.	3
Miss Winifred Shapland.	21
P. M. Sheehan, Esq.	41
E. S. Shellard, Esq.	13
F. Sheppard, Esq.	18
F. W. Showers, Esq.	10
T. L. Silvey, Esq.	37
E. V. Slade, Esq.	36
A. G. Smith, Esq.	27
Arthur G. Smith, Esq.	28
R. H. Smith, Esq.	37
W. Lints Smith, Esq.	8
F. Stamp, Esq.	3
Representative of " Star."	42
R. Stell, Esq.	34
H. B. Stone, Esq.	28
Representative of " Sunday Graphic."	42
J. H. Swallow, Esq.	23
S. Sweeney, Esq.	11

T.

	Table Number.
H. G. Tanner, Esq.	30
E. M. Tapson, Esq.	14
E. J. Taylor, Esq.	4
Sir L. Goodenough Taylor.	5
S. B. Taylor, Esq.	12
L. T. C. Thatcher, Esq.	26
The Rt. Hon. J. H. Thomas.	1
Owen Thomas, Esq.	43
Sir W. James Thomas, Bt.	6
W. J. Thomas, Esq.	24
R. Thompson, Esq.	31
T. W. Thorne, Esq.	30
Representative of " Times."	40
R. H. Todd, Esq.	5
A. C. K. Toms, Esq.	3
G. E. Turner, Esq.	36

U.

	Table Number.
T. H. J. Underdown, Esq.	15

V.

	Table Number.
E. Gwynne Vevers, Esq.	5

	Table Number.
Wallace, W. G.	~~22~~
S. E. Waday, Esq.	38
H. W. K. Wait, Esq.	5
C. S. N. Walker, Esq.	27
G. J. Walker, Esq.	11
G. A. Watkins, Esq.	27
~~H. M. Webb, Esq.~~	~~14~~
F. A. Webber, Esq.	15
H. Wheeler, Esq.	28
C. H. Whitelegge, Esq.	21
Col. Mark Whitwill.	4
H. L. Wilkinson, Esq.	17
F. C. Williams, Esq.	15
H. C. Williams, Esq.	33
Sir Watkin Williams-Wynn, Bt.	1
Willis, F. W.	15
F. O. Wills, Esq.	17
~~N. Wills, Esq.~~	~~36~~
A. M. Wilmot, Esq.	36
W. F. Wilson, Esq.	11
W. A. Winchester, Esq.	18
S. Witherington, Esq.	22
Col. H. C. Woodcock.	9
H. A. G. Worth, Esq.	12
W. T. Wright, Esq.	15
Wilshire F. A.	36
Young.	24

The big day, 31 August, arrived and the GWR had spared no expense in celebrating this milestone. A grand commemorative luncheon was held in the Great Hall of Bristol University. The 400 or so invited guests (see previous page) were treated to a no-expenses-spared slap-up lunch complemented by a 1929 Liebfraumilch, 1926 Perrier Jouet, Crofts 1917 Bristol Milk and Augier Frères 8 Star brandy. After the luncheon there were toasts to 'The King', 'The Great Western Railway' and 'The Guests'.

Guests of honour at the top table included the GWR Chairman and politician, Sir Robert Horne, Harold Macmillan MP, Lord Portal, Lord Dulverton, Marquess of Bath, Lord Mayor of Bristol, Sir James Milne (GWR General Manager), Lord Apsley and Lord Mildmay. Seated on Table 8 just in front of the top table was Mr C. B. Collett (Chief Mechanical Engineer of the GWR) and over on Table 25 was a certain Mr. F. W. Hawksworth! In addition to politicians and other GWR luminaries other guests included representatives of the national newspapers and the *Engineer* magazine and the cartoonist Mr W. Heath Robinson. The latter had just published his famous and eccentric *Railway Ribaldry* at the request of the GWR.

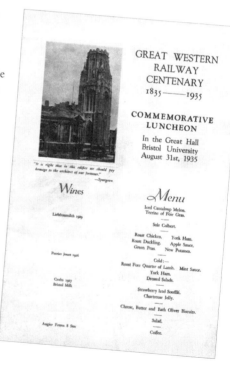

GREAT WESTERN
RAILWAY
CENTENARY
1835———1935

COMMEMORATIVE
LUNCHEON

In the Great Hall
Bristol University
August 31st, 1935

"It is right that in this edifice we should pay homage to the architect of our fortunes."
—Spurgeon.

Wines

Liebfraumilch 1929

Perrier Jouet 1926

Crofts 1917
Bristol Milk.

Augier Frères 8 Star

Menu

Iced Cantaloup Melon.
Terrine of Foie Gras.

Sole Colbert.

Roast Chicken.   York Ham.
Roast Duckling.   Apple Sauce.
Green Peas.   New Potatoes.

Cold:—
Roast Fore Quarter of Lamb.   Mint Sauce.
York Ham.
Dressed Salads.

Strawberry Iced Soufflé.
Chartreuse Jelly.

Cheese, Butter and Bath Oliver Biscuits.

Salad.

Coffee.

A METROPOLITAN TRAIN

STOP PRESS
Railway news, October 1930

The LMS are experimenting on six bridges in Derbyshire in an endeavour to discover what colour will harmonise with the surrounding landscape. Several tones of green having first been tried, the bridges have now been painted a 'battleship grey'.

The LNER Pacific No. 2795 'Call Boy' has done 28 days' continuous running between Edinburgh (Waverley) and London (King's Cross), 392¼ miles. On 24 weekdays it hauled the 'Flying Scotsman' non-stop between London and Edinburgh and on the four Sundays a day express which stops intermediately. This engine therefore covered 11.000 miles in four weeks, of which 9,400 were made up of the world's record daily non-stop run. The mileage covered by modern locomotives is frequently surprising. There is no doubt that engines are extremely hard-worked, many being double-crewed regularly.

Further engines of the 4-6-0 'Royal Scot' class have been completed at Derby. They are numbered 6152-6162. Crewe works have continued to turn out engines of the 2-6-0 mixed-traffic type, the latest being Nos. 13190 to 13203. 'Claughtons' 5905 'Lord Rathmore', 5912 'Lord Faber' and 5976 have been transferred recently to the Midland division. They had previously been adapted to the Northern division loading gauge. Most of the 2-8-0 goods engines that were built for the Somerset & Dorset Railway have been transferred to the Midland division, where they are working coal trains between Cricklewood and Toton.

STEAM LOCOMOTIVE NICKNAMES

In the early days of steam locomotives each was given a name, a practice derived from their rivals, the stage coaches. Then there were seldom two locomotives alike, but later, when four or five or more similar locos were built, they were referred to collectively by the name given to the first of the class, such as 'Precursor', or according to the main theme of names, for example, 'City' Class.

While the names of steam locomotives is a fascinating subject in itself the nicknames they were given is probably more interesting. One perfect example is the class of 2-4-2 tank locomotives designed by T. W. Wordsell for the Great Eastern Railway in 1883. These locos had an enormous appetite for coal and were duly nicknamed 'The Gobblers'. The 0-6-0 passenger tanks of the Great Eastern were called 'Jubilees' because they made their first appearance in 1897, the year of Queen Victoria's diamond jubilee.

Also on the Great Eastern the 999 class of 0-6-0 goods engines were known as 'Waterburys' because when running with steam shut off the motion made a noise which resembled the sound of a ticking clock – the Waterbury Clock Company had been making fine clocks in Waterbury, Connecticut, since 1857.

Locos of the same type on the Great Northern section were called 'Knick Knacks' for a similar reason, while the corresponding class on the old Great Central were called 'Pom Poms', from the sound of their exhaust beat.

The Great Central 'Atlantics' built at the beginning of the 20th century were considered so graceful that they were referred to as the 'Jersey Lilies', after the celebrated actress Lily Langtry. Also on the Great Central, what became the standard R.O.D. (Railway Operating Division) 2-8-0 during

World War I, Robinson's Class 8K, were so large in comparison with other locos of that period that they became affectionately known as 'Tiny'.

Nicknames could also vary widely between engine shed locations, loco crews and railway enthusiasts. The Southern Railway along with its constituent companies had its fair share of locomotive nicknames, not all of them complimentary! Stroudley's diminutive 'A1' and 'A1X' 0-6-0 tanks were known widely as 'Terriers'; Marsh's 'C2X' 0-6-0s were known as 'Dromedaries'; Drummond's 'C14' 2-2-0 tanks were 'Potato Cans'; Stroudley's 'E1' 0-6-0 tanks were 'Sea Sick Tanks'; many classes of Marsh's 4-4-2 tanks were '★anker★' Bulleid's unrebuilt 'Pacifics' were appropriately named 'Spam Cans' and his austerity 'Q1' 0-6-0s had various names such as 'Biscuit Tins', 'Coffee Pots' and 'Frankensteins' while his innovative 'Leader' class were called 'Chinese Laundries'.

There were, of course, numerous other nicknames or abbreviations given to steam locomotives. Classic examples known to railway enthusiasts of the 1950s and '60s include 'Brits', '9Fs', 'Black Fives', 'Dub Dees', 'Crabs', 'Jubes', 'Pats', 'Semis', 'Lizzies', 'Streaks' etc etc. The diesel era ushered in even more nicknames but we will draw a veil over that!

PUSH ME – PULL YOU/1
The story of the GWR's autotrains

During the 19th century the workers at the numerous mills, foundries, breweries and other manufacturing companies dotted up and down the length of the Golden Valley in Gloucestershire had to content themselves with a slow journey to work on a horse-drawn bus or on foot. Although railways had already come to the area as early as 1845 when the Cheltenham & Great Western Union Railway (later part of the GWR) opened for business, the only stations being served by the end of the century were at Chalford, Brimscombe, Stroud and Stonehouse. The proposal for an electric tramway to serve the valley spurred the GWR into action and in 1903 the company introduced a new steam railmotor on a frequent regular interval service between Chalford and Stonehouse. With new small halts eventually built along the seven-mile stretch at St Mary's Crossing, Brimscombe Bridge, Ham Mill, Bowbridge Crossing, Downfield Crossing, Cashes Green and Ebley Crossing the service was an immediate hit with local people.

Designed by G. J. Churchward the new railmotors had internally located vertical boilers and, unusually for the GWR, were fitted with outside Walschaerts valve gear. They could be driven from either end, seated 52 and had a top speed of 45mph, but were difficult to service. Soon after opening the Chalford to Stonehouse service was in such great demand that extra non-motorised trailer coaches were added but this extra weight reduced performance.

To counter this the GWR started to equip certain small classes of tank engine ('455' Class 2-4-0T, '517' Class 0-4-2T, '1076' Class 0-6-0ST/PT and '2021' Class 0-6-0ST/PT) with auto-control gear that could be operated by the driver, when the locomotive was at the rear, from a driving compartment at the front of a trailer coach. The trains, the forerunners of modern diesel multiple units, could therefore operate in a push-pull mode and the extra power greatly speeded up the service. The Golden Valley autotrain service was extended to Gloucester Central in the 1920s and other autotrains were also introduced

on some South
Wales valley lines,
the Cheltenham
to Honeybourne
route, on other
West Country
branches and on
suburban services
out of Paddington.
Some '4575' Class
2-6-2s and all
'5400' and 6400'
Class 0-6-0PTs
were also auto-

fitted at later dates and in the early 1960s could be seen operating services on
some ex-LSWR East Devon branch lines and on the Yeovil Town to Yeovil
Junction shuttle.

However, the most successful design of auto-fitted locos by far were the
'1400' Class 0-4-2Ts which were introduced in 1932 and, with their larger
driving wheels, on main-line service, such as that between Standish Junction
and Tuffley Junction which paralleled the Midland's Bristol to Gloucester main
line, could achieve speeds of 80mph.

Sadly, despite much local support, the popular autotrain service between
Chalford and Gloucester was listed for closure in the 1963 'Beeching Report'.
Headed by '1400' Class 0-4-2T No. 1472 hauling two packed autotrailers, the
last train ran on 31 October 1964 and its return journey from Chalford was
delayed by throngs of local people paying their last respects at every station and
halt along the line. The author, who was on this train, can vividly remember
some enthusiasts helping themselves to rather lengthy halt nameboards as
souvenirs! Fortunately four members of the '1400' Class along with many
autotrailers have since been preserved.

NAMED TRAINS
The Pines Express

The opening of the Somerset & Dorset Railway's northern extension to Bath in 1874 allowed through trains to travel over the London & North Western Railway and Midland Railway between the Midlands, the North of England and Bournemouth. The forerunner of what became known as 'The Pines Express', a Manchester to Bournemouth restaurant car train, first started running on weekdays throughout the year from 1 October 1910. It ceased running during World War I but was reinstated and by 1922 the train included through carriages from Bournemouth West and Swanage to Liverpool (Lime Street) and Manchester (London Road), the 248½-mile journey from Bournemouth to Manchester taking 6hrs 25min.

Running via Birmingham (New Street), Gloucester (Eastgate), Mangotsfield and Bath (Green Park) this train was given the name 'The Pines Express' in 1927 and it continued to run until the outbreak of World War II in September 1939. The 'Pines' was restored in 1949 and included a Sheffield portion except on summer Saturdays when this became a separate train. However, the journey time of 7hrs 7min by 1958 hardly meant that the train was an 'express' and was significantly slower than the same journey 36 years before. The virtual takeover of the S&D by the Western Region in 1958 spelt the end for through workings over the line and the last 'Pines' over the S&D ran on 8 September 1962 and was appropriately hauled single-handedly by BR Standard Class 9F 2-10-0 No. 92220 'Evening Star'. After that date the train was rerouted to run via Oxford and Basingstoke – the weekday train now taking 7hrs 11min between Bournemouth West and Manchester Piccadilly. The last ever 'Pines Express' over this new route ran on 4 March 1967.

After World War II the 'Pines' was normally hauled by 'Jubilee' or 'Black Five' 4-6-0s between Manchester and Bath Green Park. These were replaced by BR Sulzer Type 4s in the early 1960s but the route south from Bath was a different kettle of fish. The steeply graded line over the Mendips necessitated double-heading of the train until the introduction of BR Standard Class 9F 2-10-0s in 1960 and loco combinations on a summer Saturday were unique anywhere on BR. Pairings of ex-LMS Class 2P 4-4-0s, S&DJR Class '7F' 2-8-0s, Stanier Black Five 4-6-0s, SR 'West Country' and 'Battle of Britain' 4-6-2s, elderly Johnson Class '3F' 0-6-0s, Fowler '4F' 0-6-0s and BR Standard Class 5MT 4-6-0s were a common sight between Bath Green Park and Evercreech Junction. While the '9Fs' were the first locomotives able to haul heavy passenger trains over the Mendips without assistance their arrival on the scene came too late to save the line from closure.

Table 21

The Pines Express
AND OTHER
THROUGH TRAIN SERVICES
between
MANCHESTER, LIVERPOOL
and
CHELTENHAM, GLOUCESTER, BATH, BOURNEMOUTH
WEEKDAYS ONLY

NORTH TO SOUTH

	SX am	SX am	SO am	SO am	SO SO am	SO SO am	FO pm
Manchester Piccadilly .... dep	10 30		10 25	10 38	...	11 7	10c28 / 10e48
Stockport Edgeley .... "	10 41					10 55	A am
Liverpool Lime Street .... "		10 15				10 25	
Crewe .... "	11 19				11 40		1 24
Birmingham New Street .... "	12 45		pm				pm / 3 45
Cheltenham Spa Lansdown .... arr	1 43		2 23			pm / 3 55	
Gloucester Eastgate .... "	3 3		3 25			5 8	
Bath Green Park .... "	3 3					5 18	
Shepton Mallet Charlton Rd. .... "	4 5		4 26			5 30	
Evercreech Junction .... "						5 38	
Wincanton .... "			4 55			5 6	
Templecombe .... "						6 9	
Stalbridge .... "						6 20	
Sturminster Newton .... "			5 20			6 42	
Shillingstone .... "	4 53		5 43			6 53	
Blandford Forum .... "	5 12		5 8			7 5	6 31
Broadstone .... "	5 20						6 44
Poole .... "	5 32						
Bournemouth West .... "							

SOUTH TO NORTH

	SO am	SX am	SO am	SO am
Bournemouth West .... dep	9 15	9 45	9 45	10 32
Parkstone .... "	9 32			10 41
Poole .... "	9 39	9 54	9 54	11 15
Blandford Forum .... "	10 7	10 19	10 19	11 28 / 11 30
Sturminster Newton .... "				11 50
Stalbridge .... "		10 40		pm / 12 3
Wincanton .... "				12 20
Evercreech Junction .... "	10 52	11 6		
Shepton Mallet Charlton Rd. .... "		11 18		1 5
Bath Green Park .... "	11 50	pm / 12 1		2 20
Gloucester Eastgate .... "	pm / 1 0	12 57		2 41
Cheltenham Spa Lansdown .... arr	1 20	1 15		3 42 / 3 53 / 3 54
King's Norton .... arr		2 18		
Birmingham New Street .... "	3 55	3 43		
Crewe .... "		4 9		
Hartford .... "	4 17	4 20		
Runcorn .... "	4 38	4 44		
Liverpool Lime Street .... "	4 49	4 16		6 19 / 6448
Winslow .... "		4 25	5 25	
Stockport Edgeley .... "	4 38	4 38	5 40	
Manchester Piccadilly .... "	5 47			

† Stops only to set down passengers.
SO—Saturdays only.   SX—Saturdays excepted.
e—Stockport Tiviot Dale

A—Via Stoke-on-Trent (depart 11.55 pm).   c—Manchester Central   d—Manchester Victoria.   FO—Fridays only.

Seats on these trains may be reserved in advance from Manchester, Liverpool and Bournemouth on payment of a fee of 2s. 9d. per seat.

trains over the Mendips without assistance their arrival on the scene came too late to save the line from closure.

GLOW IN THE DARK
How nuclear power stations saved some country branch lines

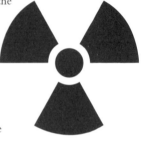

Seen as the answer to all of our energy problems, the first commercial nuclear power station started operating in Britain in 1956. Requiring vast amounts of water all of these power stations (apart from Trawsfynned in North Wales) are located on the coast or by large river estuaries. The still active nuclear waste from these facilities is transported by rail in specially designed flasks to Sellafield on the Cumbrian coast where it is reprocessed. Nuclear waste from overseas is also processed here.

Carried on a specially adapted bogie wagon, each flask weighs 50 tonnes and contains no more than 2.5 tonnes of spent nuclear fuel. The flasks have been designed to withstand a crash or a fire, one being tested in a simulated head on crash on the Old Dalby Test Track in 1984 using a remotely controlled Class 46 diesel.

Nuclear waste trains are currently operated by Direct Rail Services which was specifically created for such operations by British Nuclear Fuels in 1995. Based at Carlisle Kingmoor depot, its locomotive fleet of Class 37, 47 and 66 diesels can also be seen hauling normal freightliner trains, aggregate trains and Network Rail sandite trains.

As the nuclear flasks all travel by rail to Sellafield nearly every power station is rail connected, sometimes by a short siding linked to the nearby main line but in many cases utilising long-forgotten branch lines. Many of the older nuclear power stations have gone past their 'sell-by' date and are currently being decommissioned although the overgrown railway track still remains in situ.

The following is a list (clockwise around the coast of Britain) of the UK's nuclear power stations, both active and decommissioned, other nuclear facilities and their rail connections.

Dounreay (closed)
Exchange siding at Thurso station on ex-Highland Railway branch from Georgemas Junction. Branch still open for passengers.

Torness
Short siding from East Coast Main Line southeast of Dunbar.

Hartlepool
Ex-North Eastern Railway branch line from Seaton Carew to Seaton Snook.

Sizewell
Ex-Great Eastern Railway branch line from Saxmundham to Aldeburgh as far as Leiston.

Bradwell (closed)
Exchange siding at Southminster on ex-GER branch from Wickford. Branch still open for passengers.

Dungeness
Ex-South Eastern & Chatham Railway branch line from Appledore to Dungeness.

Winfrith (closed)
Short siding from ex-LSWR Bournemouth to Weymouth main line to the west of Wool.

Devonport Dockyard (RN nuclear submarines)
Short branch line from ex-GWR main line near Keyham station.

Hinckley Point
Exchange siding at Bridgwater.

Oldbury/Berkeley (closed)
Exchange siding at Berkeley station on ex-Severn & Wye Joint Railway branch line from Berkeley Road to Sharpness. Line still in situ.

Trawsfynydd (closed)
Exchange siding located at the site of Trawsfynndd Lake Halt on ex-GWR line from Blaenau Ffestiniog to Bala. Nuclear flask trains to and from Trawsfynydd also used the ex-LNWR Conwy Valley line from Llandudno Junction to Blaenau Ffestiniog and probably saved this scenic line from closure.

Wylfa
Exchange siding at Valley station, Anglesey, on ex-LNWR main line to Holyhead.

Heysham
Exchange siding at Heysham on ex-MR branch line from Morecambe and Lancaster.

Barrow-in-Furness
Exchange siding at Ramsden Dock to transport nuclear waste brought by ship from abroad. Reached via short ex-Furness Railway branch line from Salthouse Junction between Barrow and Roose stations.

Calder Hall (closed) and Sellafield
Exchange sidings off ex-Furness Railway Cumbrian Coast line northwest of Ravenglass station. The scenic Cumbrian Coast line was almost certainly saved from closure because of its importance to Sellafield.

Hunterston
Short siding off ex-Glasgow & South Western Railway's branch line to Largs south of Fairlie station.

WHO WAS THAT MAN?
Some famous named engines and their namesakes

The practice of naming steam locomotives started in the early days of the railways but by the early 20th century had started to take on a whole new meaning with companies such as the GWR leading the way. Soon whole classes of locomotives were being named after military leaders and heroes, regiments, football clubs, North Country hunts, saints, earls, poets, playwrights, Arthurian legends, royalty, warships, aircraft types, merchant shipping companies, locomotive designers, railway chief mechanical engineers, racehorses, seabirds, abbeys, lochs, glens, schools, cities, counties and baronial piles such as castles, halls, granges and manors. Even names of villages adorned the Isle of Wight's locomotives. The public loved it (they still do), the names adding to the romantic vision of railway travel to far off places. However standardised, many of these names were quite often of famous men (not too many women apart from royalty and the odd 'Boadicea', 'Lady Godiva' or a couple of Arthurian legend names ever appeared to adorn locomotives) that were dropped in at unexpected places. Many of these names were obviously railway officials but others are a bit harder to fathom out. Here are some examples of both (some obvious, some not so) as seen running during the BRs era. Extremely obvious names such as 'Isambard Kingdom Brunel', 'Sir Nigel Gresley' etc have been omitted for space reasons!

FORMER GWR LOCOS
'Castle' Class 4-6-0

No. 5066 'Sir Felix Pole' – (1877-1956) General Manager of the GWR, 1921-1929.

No. 5070 'Sir Daniel Gooch' – (1816-1889) First Locomotive Superintendent for GWR, 1837-1864; Chairman, 1865-1889.

No. 7000 'Viscount Portal' – (1885-1949) Last Chairman of GWR, 1945-1948.

No. 7001 'Sir James Milne' – 1883-1958) General Manager of GWR, 1929-1947.

FORMER SR LOCOS
'Battle of Britain' Class 4-6-2

No. 34052 'Lord Dowding' – (1882-1970) Commander of RAF Fighter Command during Battle of Britain.

No. 34053 'Sir Keith Park' – (1893-1975) A New Zealander and Air Chief Marshal of RAF during World War II.

No. 34054 'Lord Beaverbrook' (1879-1964) Of Canadian origin, a wealthy newspaper owner and Minister of Aircraft Production and Minister of Supply during World War II.

No. 34058 'Sir Frederick Pile' – (1884-1976) General Officer Commanding Anti-Aircraft Command during World War II.

No. 34059 'Sir Archibald Sinclair' – (1890-1970) Secretary of State for Air during World War II.

No. 34090 'Sir Eustace Missenden' – (1886-1973) Last General Manager of the Southern Railway, 1941-1948; first Chairman of the Railway Executive, 1948-1951.

No. 34109 'Sir Trafford Leigh-Mallory' – (1892-1944) Commander-in-Chief of Fighter Command, 1942; Commander-in-Chief of Allied Expeditionary Forces, 1943-1944; killed in a plane crash in the French Alps.

FORMER LMS LOCOS
'Patriot' Class 4-6-0

No. 45530 'Sir Frank Ree' – General Manager of LNWR, 1909-1914.

No. 45531 'Sir Frederick Harrison' – (1844-1914) General Manager of the London & North Western Railway, 1893-1909.

No. 45533 'Lord Rathmore' – (1838-1919) Irish-born politician and lawyer, Chairman of North London Railway and director of Central London Railway.

No. 45534 'E. Tootal Broadhurst' – (1855-1922) Cotton manufacturer; High Sheriff of Lancashire, 1906; LNWR Director.

No. 45535 'Sir Herbert Walker K.C.B.' – (1868-1949) District Superintendent of LNWR (North Wales, 1893-1902, then Euston, 1902-1912); General Manager of the London & South Western Railway, 1912-1917; acting Chairman of Railway Executive Committee during latter stages of World War I; Director of Southern Railway, 1937-1947.

No. 45536 'Private W. Wood. V.C.' - (1897-1982) Born in Stockport. Won VC in 1918 when, as a private in the 10th Battalion The Northumberland Fusiliers in fighting near Casa Vana in Italy, he single-handedly destroyed a German machine gun post and caused 140 men to surrender.

No. 45537 'Private E. Sykes V.C.' – (1885-1949) Born in Mossley, Lancashire. Worked for LNWR. Served in France and Flanders with Tyneside Irish Brigade of the 27th Battalion of the Northumberland Fusiliers. Awarded VC in 1917 for 'most conspicuous bravery and devotion to duty near Arras on 19 April'.

No. 45539 'E.C. Trench' - LNWR Director.

No. 45540 'Sir Robert Turnbull' – General Manager of LNWR, 1914.

FORMER LNER LOCOS
'A4' Class 4-6-2

No. 60001 'Sir Ronald Matthews' – (1885-1959) Chairman of the LNER; Chairman of Brush.

No. 60003 'Andrew K. McCosh' – (1880-1950) Minister of Supply, 1939-1942; Director of LNER.

No, 60004 'William Whitelaw' – (1868-1948) Chairman of Highland Railway, 1902-1912; Chairman North British Railway, 1912-1923; Chairman of LNER, 1923-1938; grandfather of William Whitelaw, Tory politician in Margaret Thatcher's Government.

No. 60005 'Sir Charles Newton' – (1882-1973) GWR 1897-1916; Great Eastern Railway 1916-1923; Chief Accountant LNER, 1928; Chief General Manager of LNER, 1939-1947.

No. 60006 'Sir Ralph Wedgwood' – (1874-1956) Chief Officer of LNER, 1923-1939, Chairman of wartime Railway Executive Committee, 1939-1941.

No. 60026 'Miles Beevor' – (1900-1994) Chief legal advisor for the LNER, 1943-1947; acting chief General Manager of LNER, 1947; Chief Secretary and legal advisor for British Transport Commission, 1947-1951; Managing Director of Brush, 1954-1958.

No. 60034 'Lord Faringdon' – (1850-1934) Railway financier and Chairman of Great Central Railway, 1889-1922.

Peppercorn 'A1' Class 4-6-2

No. 60114 'W.P. Allen' – (1888-1958) Joined GNR as cleaner at Hornsey, later General Secretary of ASLEF.

'A2/3' Class 4-6-2

No. 60500 'Edward Thompson' – (1881-1954) Mechanical Engineer at Stratford Works, 1930-1941; Chief Mechanical Engineer of LNER, 1941-1946.

'B1' Class 4-6-0

Seventeen of this class were named after LNER directors. Here are some of the more interesting ones:

No. 61238 'Leslie Runciman' – (1900-1989) Shipping magnate (Walter Runciman & Co); First Director-General of British Overseas Airways

Corporation, 1939-1943; Deputy Chairman of Lloyds Bank, 1962-1971; Director of LNER.

No. 61241 'Viscount Ridley' – (1902-1964) British peer (3rd Viscount Ridley), the son of Matthew White Ridley (1874-1916, 2nd Viscount) who was MP for Stalybridge, 1900-1904; Director of LNER.

No. 61243 'Sir Harold Mitchell' – (1900-1983) Born in Fife; MP for Brentford and Chiswick, 1931-1945; Vice-Chairman of Conservative Party; British peer; many business interests around the world including coal mines, glass works and shipping; Director of LNER.

No. 61244 'Strang Steel' – (1882-1961) MP for Ashford, 1918-1929; Lord Lieutenant of Selkirkshire, 1948-1953; Director of LNER.

No. 61245 'Murray of Elibank' – (1877-1951) 2nd Viscount Elibank; served as diplomat in overseas territories, 1898-1917; MP for Glasgow St Rollox, 1918-1922; Lord Lieutenant of Peeblesshire, 1939-1945; Honorary Colonel of 8th Battalion The Royal Scots, 1939-1945; Director of LNER.

No. 61246 'Lord Balfour of Burleigh' – (1883-1967) 7th Lord Balfour of Burleigh (of Burleigh Castle, Kinross); Scottish Representative Peer, 1922-1963; Director of LNER. His father, the 6th Lord (1849-1921), served as Parliamentary Secretary to the Board of Trade, 1888-1892; Secretary for Scotland, 1895-1903; Governor of Bank of Scotland, 1904-1921.

No. 61250 'A. Harold Bibby' – (1889-1986) Liverpool shipping magnate; High Sheriff of Cheshire, 1934-1935; Chairman of Bibby Line, 1932-1969; Director of various maritime insurance companies; Governor of Rugby School, 1932-1967; Director of Suez Canal Company, 1939-1957; Director of LNER.

No. 61251 'Oliver Bury' – (1861-1946) English railway engineer with business interests in South America; Chief Mechanical Engineer on the Great Western Railway of Brazil; General Manager of Great Northern Railway, 1902-1923; Director of LNER, 1923-1945.

A–Z OF LONDON'S MAIN RAILWAY STATIONS

Blackfriars

Opened as St Paul's station by the London, Chatham & Dover Railway on 10 May 1886. Renamed 'Blackfriars' on 1 February 1937. Rebuilt 1970s. Currently being rebuilt again. Effectively a through station served by Thameslink trains between Bedford and Brighton via Snow Hill Tunnel.

Platforms: 2

Current passenger usage: 12,959,108

Broad Street

Opened by North London Railway on 1 November 1865. Extended in 1891 and 1913. Damaged during World War I and World War II. Closed 30 June 1986. Demolished and site redeveloped.

Platforms: 9

Cannon Street

Original building designed by John Wolfe Barry and Sir John Hawkshaw, opened by South Eastern Railway on 1 September 1866. Badly damaged during World War II. Redeveloped 1958 – present day. Threatened with closure in 1980s.

Platforms: 7

Current passenger usage: 21,646,380

Charing Cross

Built on site of Hungerford Market. Original building designed by Sir John Hawkshaw, opened by South Eastern Railway on 11 January 1864. Roof collapsed 1905. Redeveloped 1990s.

Platforms: 6
Current passenger usage: 36,659,932

Euston

Original building and Doric Arch designed by Philip Hardwick, opened by London & Birmingham Railway 20 July 1837. Enlarged in 1849 with Great Hall designed by Philip Charles Hardwick. Demolished amidst great public protest in 1961-2 and replaced by new building opened in 1968.
Platforms: 18
Current passenger usage: 27,499,986

Fenchurch Street

Replaced terminus at Minories opened on 6 July 1840. Original station designed by William Tite, opened by London & Blackwall Railway on 20 July 1841. Rebuilt 1854 to design by George Berkeley. Became London terminus of London, Tilbury & Southend Railway in 1858.
Platforms: 4
Current passenger usage: 15,675,602

Holborn Viaduct

Opened by London, Chatham & Dover Railway on 2 March 1874. Operated as a through station until 1916 when passenger trains through Snow Hill Tunnel were withdrawn. Closed on 26 January 1990.
Platforms: 6

King's Cross

Built on the site of a fever and smallpox hospital. Designed by Lewis Cubitt and opened by Great Northern Railway on 14 October 1852. Replaced temporary terminus at Maiden Lane; opened on 7 August 1850. Building currently being restored. Famous for its new Platform 0 and the fictional Platform 9¾ which features in the 'Harry Potter' books and films.

Platforms: 12
Current passenger usage: 24,641,427

Liverpool Street

Built on site of Bethlem Royal Hospital ('Bedlam'). Designed by Edward
Wilson, opened by GER on 2 February 1874. Replaced original terminus at
Bishopsgate; opened by Eastern Counties Railway on 1 July 1840.
Platforms: 18
Current passenger usage: 55,103,416

London Bridge

Two separate stations with the first being the earliest railway terminus to open
in London.

Original station opened by London & Greenwich Railway on 14 December
1836. Adjacent separate station opened by London & Croydon Railway on 5
June 1839, later also used by London & Brighton Railway in 1841, followed
by South Eastern Railway in 1842. The two adjoining stations then swapped
owners with the original station (now under the control of the L&CR, L&BR

and the SER) being rebuilt and reopened in 1844.

In 1846 the L&CR and L&BR merged to form the London, Brighton & South Coast Railway. The LB&SCR went on to demolish the five-year-old former joint station in 1849 and replace it with a new enlarged station which was completed in 1854. It was again enlarged with a single-span arched glass roof in 1862.

In the meantime, the adjacent (original L&GR) station had already been taken over by the South Eastern Railway who rebuilt and enlarged it between 1847-1850, allowing the company to close its former terminus at Bricklayer's Arms. The station was again rebuilt in 1864 to allow their trains to travel to Charing Cross and also in 1866 for trains to Cannon Street. The SER and the London, Chatham & Dover Railway merged in 1899 to form the South Eastern & Chatham Railway.

The two stations at London Bridge came under the ownership of the newly formed Southern Railway in 1923 and by World War II nearly all train services out of the two stations had been electrified. Suffering severe damage during the war, the stations were later redeveloped in the 1970s. Further expansion to accommodate longer trains is scheduled to start soon.

Platforms: 15

Current passenger usage: 49,703,152

Marylebone

Designed by Henry Braddock. Opened by Great Central Railway on 15 March 1899. Mainline services northwards to Nottingham ceased on 3 September 1966. Restoration in 1980s.

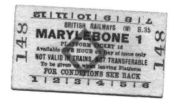

Platforms: 6

Current passenger usage: 11,396,645

Paddington

Temporary terminus opened by Great Western Railway on 4 June 1838. Designed by Isambard Kingdom Brunel and Matthew Digby Wyatt, the current terminus opened on 29 May 1854. Enlarged 1906–1915. Damaged during World War II. The dedicated Heathrow Express which first ran in 1998 is the only electrified service using the station.

Platforms: 14

Current passenger usage: 29,302,758

St Pancras

Built on site of slums and a churchyard. Designed by George Gilbert Scott, opened by Midland Railway on 1 October 1868. Damaged during World War II. Escaped demolition in the 1960s and was restored to its former glory in the early 21st century. Also terminus for Eurostar high-speed trains to Paris and Brussels via the Channel Tunnel since 2007.

Platforms: 15

Current passenger usage (including King's Cross Thameslink station):
17,462,297

Victoria

Essentially two stations. West side opened by London, Brighton & South Coast Railway on 1 October 1860. Rebuilt 1898-1908. East side opened by London, Chatham & Dover Railway on 25 August 1862 (shared by GWR broad gauge trains from Southall via West London Extension Joint Railway until they ceased in 1866). Rebuilt by South Eastern & Chatham Railway, reopened 16 June 1906. Two stations made into one by Southern Railway in 1923 but today still effectively operates as two separate stations.

Platforms: 19

Current passenger usage: 70,157,115

Waterloo

Built on arches above marshy ground near River Thames. Original station designed by William Tite, opened by London & South Western Railway on 11 July 1848. Extended 1878-1885. Rebuilt 1899-1922. Damaged during World War II. Became temporary terminus for Eurostar trains from 1994-2007. UK's busiest station.

Platforms: 19 (+5 in disused Eurostar terminal)

Current passenger usage: 87,930,076

NOTE: Passenger usage figures are taken from total of entries and exits for 2008/9 and exclude similar figures for adjoining Underground stations.

THE OLD SLOW & DIRTY LIVES ON
Railway activities along the closed Somerset & Dorset Joint Railway

Its loss greatly mourned by local people and railway enthusiasts alike, the Somerset & Dorset Joint Railway was finally put to sleep after years of deliberate neglect on 7 March 1966 – the line saw its last trains, both enthusiasts' specials, on the previous day. For years the railway disappeared into the landscape, slowly being overtaken by nature. Fear not, however, as all is not lost, with many green shoots of recovery now sprouting up along the line. Here are the highlights from north to south:

Bath Green Park station
The restored vaulted glass roof and station building survive next to a supermarket. It provides a covered space for markets and events. The booking office is now a restaurant.

Devonshire Tunnel, Combe Down Tunnel, Tucking Mill Viaduct and Midford Viaduct
Trackbed now in the process of being converted by Sustrans for the 'Two Tunnels Greenway' footpath and cycleway due to open throughout in 2012. Will form part of the National Cycle Network Route 24 which also takes in the route of the closed ex-GWR line from Radstock to Frome.

Midsomer Norton station
Now owned by the Somerset & Dorset Railway Heritage Trust who have restored the station and platforms, built a replica signal box and are currently relaying track southwards towards Masbury. Diesel-hauled brake van rides are run

at weekends. Long-term plans include introducing a steam locomotive and relaying the track to Chilcompton.

Charlton Viaduct, Shepton Mallet
This Grade II listed 27-arch viaduct now forms the impressive backdrop to Kilver Court Gardens that were originally developed by Showerings, the manufacturer of Babycham. The gardens, also known as the 'Secret Garden of Somerset', are open to the public throughout the year.

Trackbed of original 'main line' west of Glastonbury
Much of the trackbed is now a 5-mile footpath and cycleway from the western outskirts of Glastonbury to Ashcott (refreshments at the quaint 'Railway Inn') and Shapwick. The route passes through several nature reserves formed from old peat workings, popular with birdwatchers throughout the year.

Yenston, south of Templecombe
The 2ft gauge Gartell Light Railway now runs southwards from Yenston along about one mile of the S&D trackbed. Both steam and diesel-hauled trains operate on this fully signalled line on selected Sundays during the summer.

Shillingstone station
The main station building and platform have been restored by the Shillingstone Railway Project and are open to the public at weekends and on Wednesdays. Current plans include relaying a half-mile of track. BR Standard Class 9F 2-10-0 No. 92207 is currently being restored here.

WARTIME FACTS AND FIGURES
How Britain's railways helped to defeat Hitler

O n 1 September 1939, the Government took control of all the standard gauge railways in Britain. This was done by the issue of an Order under the Emergency Powers (Defence) Act, 1939 on behalf of the Minister of Transport. Fixed annual payments were then made by the Government in exchange for the net revenues of the railway operating companies.

The fixed annual payments were as follows:
Great Western Railway £6,670,603
London & North Eastern Railway £10,136,355
London, Midland & Scottish Railway £14,749,698
Southern Railway £6,607,639
London Passenger Transport Board £4,835,705
Minor railways £500,000

The wartime task of Britain's railways was immense and made even more difficult by the conditions under which they had to operate. Blackouts, bombing, lack of maintenance and overworked staff all added to the burden. The statistics are staggering, proving that the indispensable role of the railways during World War II was a key factor in the final victory of the Allies over Nazi Germany in 1945.

- In the first three years of the war the mileage run by trains operated by mainline railways was 1,265,000,000.
- In performing the above task locomotives ran 1,870,000,000 miles.
- Mainline railway passenger travel in 1942 totalled 30,000,000,000 miles, an increase of 50% on pre-war mileage. At the same time there was a reduction of 28% in the mileage run by passenger trains: thus the loading of the trains more than doubled.

- All of the additional traffic meant that locomotives had to do much more work than in peacetime. They spent 7,000,000 (or 11%) more hours in traffic, while the number available for actual work had, up to the end of 1942, increased by less than 1%.
- The British Expeditionary Force moving to ports of embarkation in 1939 involved the Southern Railway in running 1,100 special trains for 390,000 personnel plus other special trains for stores and ammunition.
- The Norway expedition needed 202 special trains run by one railway alone.
- For the 319,116 troops evacuated from Dunkirk in 1940, 620 special trains were run in 16 days.
- First exports to Russia involved one railway in running 132 special trains between August and November 1941.
- Nearly one million loaded wagons were being forwarded on Britain's railways each week. Compared with 1938, the miles they covered increased in 1942 by nearly 1,000,000,000. Freight trains became longer, each carrying an extra 13% of wagons.
- Each year practically the whole of Britain's 4,500,000-ton grain harvest was carried by rail to storage depots and to mills.
- The whole war effort depended on the production and distribution of coal; 80% of coal mined in Britain was carried by the railways. In 1942 this amounted to 160,750,000 tons.
- In 1938 some 20% of the 227,000,000 tons of coal mined was exported. By

1943 this had dropped to only 3.26%. Export coal involved short rail hauls and much longer hauls were needed to feed the home market, where the balance of export coal then went. The average coal train haul rose from 46 pre-war miles to 63 miles by 1943.

• The railways also served war factories. By 1944 nearly 7,000 special trains were run every day to carry workers to Government factories alone. Millions of other workers travelled by rail to other factories. In one year 385,000,000 passenger journeys were made by holders of workmen's tickets.

• Factory construction required rail connections and rail transport, for both the input of raw materials and the output of finished secret lethal products. As the output increased so the rail services had to be enlarged. For one factory alone (somewhere in Britain!) 58 trains were run each day; at the peak period ten trains departed in 20 minutes.

• During the war the volume of civilian travel on the railways continued at a high level despite there being fewer trains. Overcrowding and standing room only was the norm. Absolute priority was given to trains for the services and for workmen in factories. Locomotives, normally used to haul passenger trains, were hauling war traffic while smaller locos were doing the work of larger types – both hauling loads to the limit of their capacity.

• During the first evacuations of children and civilians from the London area the railways ran 4,349 trains carrying 1,428,425 passengers. Against the threat of invasion, a complete scheme was prepared for the evacuation of the entire civil population from areas in the East and South coasts. Thirty-eight trains were run for

14,600 Dutch, Belgian and French refugees seeking sanctuary in Britain.

- During the Blitz on London, tube stations were be used by the public seeking shelter. Seventy-nine deep level stations were fitted with bunks, special sanitary equipment and clinics along with 124 canteen points to which 11 tons of food was delivered daily by special trains. During the early days of the Blitz 177,000 civilians took shelter each night on the Underground. Other shelter accommodation was also provided for 14,000 civilians in disused tunnels and closed stations.

- In preparation for the Allied landings in North Africa in 1942, in one month alone 185,000 men, 20,000 vehicles and 220,000 tons of stores were carried by rail to the ports. This involved the running of 440 troop trains, 680 freight trains and 15,000 wagons by ordinary goods service.

- British locomotives were also sent abroad to support fighting fronts. Many sent out with the BEF to France in 1939 were lost after Dunkirk. Sent overseas to the Near East were 143 heavy freight locomotives (along with 1,600 goods wagons) where they operated in Syria and Persia. The first locomotive to enter El Alamein after its recapture was of LMS design; LNER locos went to work on the Haifa-Beirut-Triploi line, while a GWR loco was seen at work in Tunisia.

- The Luftwaffe attack on Coventry on 14 November 1940 was made by 400 bombers. Of the 600 'incidents' reported in the city no fewer than 122 were on railway property. Coventry station, sidings, junctions, main and branch lines, bridges and viaducts were all hit. One 3½-mile stretch of line received 40 high-explosive bombs. So well did the engineers and the gangs do their work that by the evening of the 16th both the Coventry to Birmingham and Coventry to Leamington lines were clear.

- During the war women played an important part in keeping Britain's railways moving. They took over many jobs normally carried out by men including maintenance of locomotives and rolling stock, working on the permanent way, making concrete sleepers, crane operators, signalwomen, guards, motor van drivers, woodworking and metalworking.

SOUTHERN RAILWAY FAMOUS TRAINS

The Bournemouth Belle

Pullman cars had been used on the London & South Western Railway since the late 19th century. These were single cars attached to scheduled services and they had gone out of fashion by 1911. However, other railway companies in southern England, such as the London Brighton & South Coast Railway's 'Pullman Limited' and the 'Southern Belle' between Victoria and Brighton, were having more success. These all-Pullman trains became part of the Southern Railway in the 1923 Grouping and their success led the company to experiment with a similar train between Waterloo and Bournemouth. The 'Bournemouth Belle' first ran in 1931 but only operated on summer Sundays until 1936 when it became a regular daily working and, apart from its suspension during World War II, continued to run until its demise in 1967.

In its pre-war years the 'Belle' was usually hauled by a 'Lord Nelson' 4-6-0 and travelled non-stop between Waterloo and Southampton before calling at Bournemouth Central and terminating at Bournemouth West. Following the end of the war the train was reinstated in 1947 but this time it was hauled by one of Bulleid's new 'Merchant Navy' Class 4-6-2s. So popular was the train that it often extended to 12 carriages with a total weight of nearly 500 tons, a load just within the 'Merchant Navy's' capability.

By 1963 the 79¼ miles between Waterloo and Southampton Central were being covered in 1hr 21min with arrival at Bournemouth Central exactly 2hrs after departure from London – an average speed of 54mph for the 108-mile journey. Hardly an express!! Steam clung on to life on the route until the summer of 1967 providing the 'Merchant Navy' locos with their swan song. The 'Belle', for the last few months diesel-hauled, last ran on 9 July when third-rail electrification was switched on.

The Devon Belle

Unlike the 'Bournemouth Belle' and the all-electric 'Brighton Belle', the 'Devon Belle' had an extremely short existence. Hauled by the latest 'Merchant Navy' Class 4-6-2s as far as Exeter Central, this all-Pullman train first ran in June 1947. Departing from Waterloo at 12 noon the 12 or 14-coach train was officially non-stop to Sidmouth Junction but, in fact, engines were changed out of sight at Wilton to the west of Salisbury – the only train booked to run non-stop through Salisbury since an accident there in 1906. At Exeter, the second 'Merchant Navy' came off and the train was split with one portion going on to Ilfracombe and the other to Plymouth. Bulleid's new light Pacifics were ideal locomotives for this second leg of the journey although banking assistance was always needed up the steep Braunton Bank and on the return out of Ilfracombe.

Unusually the Ilfracombe portion of the train carried an observation car at the rear. This was not the first time such cars had been used in Britain – the short-lived 'Coronation' run by the LNER before the war carried an observation car and after the war these were used on Highland tourist routes in Scotland. Paying a supplement, observation car passengers on the 'Devon Belle' must have had a wonderful close-up view of the banking engine as the train struggled up the 1 in 36 Braunton Bank between Barnstaple and Ilfracombe.

Sadly, patronage of the Plymouth portion was poor and this was discontinued in 1949 leaving the summer-only 'Belle' as a Waterloo–Ilfracombe service until September 1954 when it, too, was withdrawn. In 1961 the observation cars saw service on the Inverness to Kyle of Lochalsh line and the Glasgow to Oban line. Fortunately both of them have survived and can be seen in action on the Paignton & Dartmouth Railway and the Swanage Railway respectively.

STOP PRESS
Railway news, July 1933

Work has been well maintained on the new 4-6-2 'Pacific' express locomotives now in hand at Crewe and the first is almost completed. It is numbered 6200. Nine more 3-cylinder 4-6-0 locomotives of the 'Baby Scot' class have been turned out from Derby works, so completing the batch of 10 constructed there.

Big parties visiting the GWR locomotive works at Swindon are to be given the opportunity of seeing the engine testing plant in full working order, as this is now included in the programme of the tour of the works. The plant is the only one of its kind in the country and on it engines may be tested at a speed of 70mph while remaining stationary, the driving wheels running on wheels in the plant instead of on rails.

The LMSR are about to make extensive trials of heavy oil traction. In addition to the 0-6-0 shunting locomotives, fitted with a 400hp heavy oil engine, which has been constructed in the company's workshops and is now undergoing tests, 11 shunting locomotives are being obtained from outside manufacturers. Three of these will have the 0-4-0 wheel arrangement, the remainder being of the 0-6-0 type.

Commencing on the 17th July the 'Cornish Riviera Express' will run non-stop from Paddington to Plymouth, 225¾ miles, in 3hrs 57mins. This is 10 minutes quicker than at present. Other West of England expresses not booked to call at Westbury and Frome will be similarly accelerated. For instance the 'Torbay Express' will cover the 199¾ miles from Paddington to Torquay in 210 minutes – five minutes quicker than last year.

MADE IN SCOTLAND
The story of five railway-owned Scottish locomotive works

St Rollox

Located in Springburn, Glasgow, St Rollox Works opened in 1856 as the locomotive, carriage and wagon works for the Caledonian Railway. At the height of production in the early 20th century St Rollox works covered an area of 190 acres and employed around 5,000 men building classic steam locomotives designed by such luminaries as Dugald Drummond, John McIntosh (famous for his 'Oban Bogies', 'Dunalastair' and 'Cardean' Classes) and

William Pickersgill. During World War II the works produced Horsa gliders and parts for the Roll-Royce Merlin engine. In 1948 St Rollox became the chief locomotive works for British Railways in Scotland, overhauling steam locomotives until 1966, but, despite modernisation in the 1960s at a cost of £1.5 million, the Works had been slimmed down by the early 1980s. Today, the much-reduced facility at St Rollox is run by Railcare Ltd who maintain and overhaul rolling stock.

Cowlairs

Also located in Springburn, Glasgow, Cowlairs Works was built in 1841 for the Edinburgh & Glasgow Railway, before going on to become the main locomotive, carriage and wagon works for the North British Railway. The first two locomotives built at the works were two powerful 0-6-0 banking engines for use on the nearby in 42 Cowlairs Incline out of Queen Street station. Under the watchful eye of Chief Mechanical Engineers such as Matthew

Holmes and William Reid, Cowlairs Works turned out some classic steam locomotives culminating in Reid's famous 'Glen' Class (LNER Class 'D34') 4-4-0s which remained in service on the West Highland Line through to the BR era. Like nearby St Rollox, the Works produced Horsa gliders and parts for Rolls-Royce Merlin engines during World War II. Locomotive construction ended following the Big Four Grouping of 1923 although locomotive, carriage and wagon repair work continued through the LNER era until 1948. The works closed in 1968 and the site is now an industrial estate.

Inverurie

Located 16¾ miles north of Aberdeen, Inverurie Locomotive Works was opened in 1903 by the Great North of Scotland Railway, replacing the cramped works they had been using previously at Kittybrewster. Despite only building ten new locomotives in its lifetime the Works continued to repair locomotives and rolling stock through the LNER and BR eras until 1969 when it closed. Designed by William Pickersgill, eight of the Class

'V' and two of their Class 'F' 4-4-0s (both later classified by the LNER as Class 'D34') were built at Inverurie while the rest of these graceful locomotives were built by the North British Locomotive Company in Glasgow. One NBL loco, No. 49 'Gordon Highlander', has since been preserved.

Lochgorm

Located in the triangle of lines outside Inverness station, Lochgorm Railway Works was built by the Inverness & Nairn Railway in 1855 and became the main locomotive works for its eventual successor, the Highland Railway. Under

William Stroudley the works first turned out three diminutive 0-6-0 tanks which were the predecessors of his famous 'Terrier' tank locomotives designed for the London, Brighton & South Coast Railway. Under his successor, David Jones, Lochgorm went on to build 4-4-0 and 2-4-0 tender locos, 2-4-0 tank locos and the famous 4-4-0 'Skye Bogies'. Despite this many of the Highland Railway's locomotives such as the famous 'Jones Goods' were built by outside contractors such as Sharp, Stewart and Company, Dübs, Neilson and Hawthorn Leslie.

Jones was succeeded by Peter Drummond as the Highland Railway's locomotive superintendent. Nine of his 'Small Ben' 4-4-0s were built at Lochgorm along with three 0-6-0 tank locos and four 0-4-0 tank locos.

Lochgorm became part of the LMS in 1923 and continued to repair locomotives and rolling stock until the BR era. The works were used as a diesel maintenance and running shed following closure of Inverness steam shed in 1961.

Kilmarnock

Originally located in Glasgow, the Glasgow & South Western Railway's locomotive works was moved to Kilmarnock in 1854. Under successive locomotive superintendents such as Patrick and James Stirling, Hugh Smellie, James Manson, Peter Drummond and Robert Whitelegg, Kilmarnock produced around 400 steam locomotives for the company. Despite this many of the company's locos were built by outside contractors such as the North British Locomotive Company. From 1923 the G&SWR became part of the LMS with most of the heavy repair work being transferred to St Rollox. Loco repair work ended in 1952 with rolling stock repair ceasing in 1959. The LMS was quick to rid itself of ex-G&SWR locos with most them withdrawn by the mid-1930s.

RAILWAY JOURNEYS TRIVIA
In memory of the good old days – trivia seen, noted or heard along the way

1. Unscientific passenger census on Gloucester Central to Hereford train 18 April 1964.

Train engine '4300' Class 2-6-0 No. 6349. Note: these numbers do not include those who joined the train at Gloucester!

Oakle Street: 0 off/0 on
Grange Court: 2 off/0 on
Blaisdon Halt: 0 off/0 on
Longhope: 0 off/0 on
Mitcheldean Road: 0 off/4 on
Weston-under-Penyard: 0 off/0 on
Ross-on-Wye: 0 off/11 on
Fawley: 1 off/3 on
Ballingham: 0 off/5 on
Holme Lacy: 0 off/12 on

FOOTNOTE: The Gloucester to Hereford service ceased on 31 October 1964.

2. Edinburgh Haymarket, 30 July 1964

Q. Have you got your 'Munro Gravicon Hopper' yet?
A. No.
Reply: Well, there's one standing in Haymarket coal yard.

3. Poster at Sheringham station, 18 August 1965
Quaker Queries

Do you behave with brotherly love to all men whatever their race, background or opinion?
Do you try to make the stranger feel at home among you?

4. Cameo scenes noted on a journey between King's Lynn and Norwich, 18 August 1965

Middleton Towers – sand pits, transfer to railway wagons, private-owner 0-4-0 diesel, coal yard

East Winch – Grain? Loading chutes for transfer to railway wagons. Long goods train in refuge siding. Coal yard

Narborough & Pentney – Derelict goods shed. Private siding to factory or mill. No coal

Swaffham – Large number of full coal trucks. Loading of grain or something (?) from factory. Weeding of goods yard with hoes in progress. Coal yard. Large goods shed. Thetford line intact but rusty

Dunham, Fransham and Wendling – Loops removed. No goods facilities

5. A 'Hall' at Exeter on 1 September 1964

A rare sight indeed by then as 'Hall' Class 4-6-0 No. 6925 'Hackness Hall' headed out of Exeter St David's up the 1 in 37 incline to Central station with an eastbound cement train. It was assisted at the front by Ivatt Class 2 2-6-2T No. 41295 and at the rear by 0-6-0PTs Nos. 4610 and 4694.

6. With apologies to the Beatles

Sung to the tune of 'A Hard Day's Night' and the clickety-clack of the rail joints this little ditty was heard while travelling on a train between Perth and Glasgow Buchanan Street on 30 July 1964 (loco BR Class 5 No. 73149)

'It's been a soft day's night
And I've been resting like a cat
It's been a soft day's night
I should be waking like a twig
But when I go away from you
The things that you don't do
Make me feel all horrible
Scream aargh....'

7. The end of the world, 1 January 1966

Despite the official end of steam on the Western Region on 31 December 1965 our Gloucester-based trainspotter continued to have hallucinations for the next six months! Here are some of the poor lad's ramblings:

2 January – No. 92128 on goods

16 January – No. 48296 on goods, No. 48375 light engine

26 February – Nos. 48177 and 48669 in steam at Horton Road shed (closed to steam 31/12/65)

16 March – No. 48435 light engine going towards Gloucester

2 April – LM steam loco seen going towards Bristol at Tuffley Junction

19 June – while in bed heard steam engine travelling towards Gloucester from Barnwood

FOOTNOTE: By now a raving lunatic, our trainspotter was sedated after the last incident!

RAILWAYS THAT NEVER WERE
Proposals for new railways in Scotland

The question of rural transport in Scotland was studied by a Parliamentary Committee which published its findings in 1919. It makes interesting reading following on from earlier stillborn proposals by the Highland Railway to build new railways in the northwest of Scotland and on the islands of Lewis and Skye.

In their report the Committee advocated the building of 382 miles of new railway, 85 miles of new road, road improvements and the introduction of new bus and steamer services. As the majority of these proposed schemes would pass through sparsely populated and remote countryside the Committee pressed the point that Government funding would be necessary.

It must be remembered that at this time the UK was just starting to recover from World War I and was seriously in debt – at home there were shortages of raw materials, food and fuel, and unrest among the workforce with strikes already making themselves felt, while abroad revolution and political shockwaves were spreading around the world. However well-meaning, the Committee's cosy schemes to liberate unpopulated regions of Scotland never had a cat's chance of succeeding.

Theoretically, the majority of their new railway proposals would have been possible under the 1896 Light Railways Act, which did away with a lot of red tape and Health & Safety nonsense, enabling lines to be built and operated at less expense that normal railways. The narrow gauge lines were to be built to a 60cm gauge using German military railway equipment 'liberated' at the end of the war. The following list of these new routes is fascinating as some of them had already been proposed years before (with no success) and none, apart from the Cromarty branch which was started but not finished, were actually built.

Standard gauge lines

Culrain to Lochinver 40 miles
Garve to Ullapool 33 miles
Parton to Dalmellington 28 miles
Turriff to Maud 21½ miles
Alford to Bellabeg 19 miles
Conon to Cromarty 18 miles
Ballater to Braemar 17 miles
Stranraer to Drummore 14½ miles
Fraserburgh to Aberdour 9 miles
Lybster to Dunbeath 8 miles
Pinwherry to Ballantrae 8 miles
Balfron to Fintry 8 miles
Thurso to Scrabster 2 miles

Narrow gauge lines

Isle of Skye 75 miles
Isle of Lewis 40 miles
Dunoon to Strachur 21 miles
Isle of Arran 20 miles

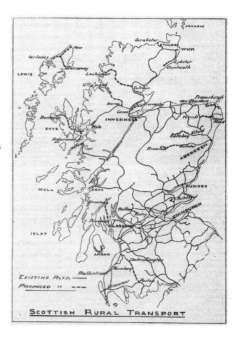

FOOTNOTE: The Committee also proposed a revolutionary new road system, constructing concrete wheel tracks either on or at the side of existing roads, and at the same level. They suggested that bye-laws should make it obligatory on motor drivers to use these tracks. The Committee recommended a test of its practicability on a stretch of road at some suitable locality. It seems they eventually got their way when £116.2 million was earmarked for the controversial Cambridgeshire Guided Busway in 2009! It follows the course of the closed Cambridge to St Ives railway but, quite frankly, it would have been cheaper to have reopened the railway.

RAILWAY MUSEUMS

Many railway museums can be found attached to heritage railways, while others range from the extensive National Railway Museum at York to the tiny Glenfinnan Station Museum in Scotland. Some local authority-run museums that include railway exhibits, such as the Manchester Museum of Science & Industry, are also included.

The West Country

Blue Anchor Railway Museum
Blue Anchor Station, Blue Anchor, Nr Minehead, Somerset, TA24 6LG
Great Western Railway Museum
The Old Railway Station, Railway Drive, Coleford, Gloucestershire,
   GL16 8RH
Lynton & Barnstaple Railway Museum
Woody Bay Station, Parracombe, Barnstaple, North Devon, EX31 4RA
Newton Abbot Town and Great Western Railway Museum
2a St Paul's Road, Newton Abbot, Devon, TQ12 2HP
Pallot Heritage Steam, Motor and General Museum
Rue de Bechet, Trinity, Jersey, Channel Islands, JE3 5BE
Purbeck Mineral & Mining Museum
Norden Station, Nr Swanage, Dorset, BH20 5DW
Somerset & Dorset Railway Trust Museum
Midsomer Norton Station, Silver Street, Midsomer Norton, Somerset,
   BA3 2EY
Somerset & Dorset Railway Trust Museum
The Railway Station, Washford, Somerset, TA23 0PP
South Devon Railway Museum
Buckfastleigh Station, Buckfastleigh, Devon. TQ11 0DZ

Steam Museum of the Great Western Railway
Kemble Drive, Swindon, SN2 2TA
Swanage Railway Museum
Corfe Castle Station, Nr Swanage, Dorset, BH20 5EJ
Tiverton Museum
Beck's Square, Tiverton, Devon, EX16 6PJ
West Somerset Railway Museum
Bishops Lydeard Station, Bishops Lydeard, Nr Taunton, Somerset, TA4 3RU
Woodspring Museum
Burlington Street, Weston-super-Mare, North Somerset, BS23 1PR

Southern England

Amberley Museum & Heritage Centre
Amberley, Nr Arundel, West Sussex, BN18 9LT
Buckingham Railway Centre
Quainton Road Station, Nr Aylesbury, Buckinghamshire, HP22 4BY
Colonel Stephens Railway Museum
Tenterden Town Station, Station Road, Tenterden, Kent, TN30 6HE
Didcot Railway Centre
Station Road, Didcot, Oxfordshire, OX11 7NJ
Isle of Wight Steam Railway
Havenstreet Station, Havenstreet, Isle of Wight, PO33 4DS
Kew Bridge Steam Museum
Green Dragon Lane, Brentford TW8 0EN
London Transport Museum
Covent Garden Piazza, London, WC2E 7BB
Pendon Museum
Long Whittenham, Abingdon, Oxfordshire, OX14 4QD

Wales

Conwy Valley Railway Museum
The Old Goods Yard, Betws-y-Coed, Conwy, LL24 0AL
Corris Railway Museum
Corris Station Yard, Corris, Nr Machynlleth, Powys, SY20 9SH
Ffestiniog Railway Museum
Harbour Station, Porthmadog, Gwynedd, LL49 9NF
Narrow Gauge Railway Museum
Wharf Station, Tywyn, Gwynedd LL36 9EY
National Slate Museum
Llanberis, Gwynedd, LL55 4TY
National Waterfront Museum
Oystermouth Road, Maritime Quarter, Swansea, SA1 3RD
Penrhyn Castle Industrial Railway Museum
Penrhyn Castle, Llandegai, Nr Bangor, Gwynedd, LL57 4HN

Midlands and East Anglia

Birmingham Railway Museum
670 Warwick Road, Tyseley, Birmingham, B11 2HL
Black Country Museum
Tipton Road, Dudley, West Midlands, DY1 4SQ
Bressingham Steam Museum
Thetford Road, Diss, Norfolk, IP22 2AB
Cheddleton Railway Centre
Cheddleton Station, Station Road, Cheddleton, Staffordshire, ST13 7EE
Crewe Heritage Centre
Vernon Way, Crewe, Cheshire, CW1 2DB
Derby Industrial Museum
19 Full Street, Derby, DE1 3AR

East Anglian Railway Museum
Chappel & Wakes Colne Station, Wakes Colne, Colchester, Essex, CO6 2DS
Irchester Narrow Gauge Museum
Irchester Country Park, Wellingborough, Northants, NN29 7DL
Ironbridge Gorge Museum
Ironbridge, Telford, Shropshire, TF8 7AW
Kidderminster Railway Museum
Station Drive, Comberton Hill, Kidderminster, Worcestershire, DY10 1QX
Mangapps Railway Museum
Southminster Road, Burnham-on-Crouch, Essex, CM0 8QG
Midland Railway Centre
Butterley Station, Ripley, Derbyshire, DE5 3QZ
Mid-Suffolk Light Railway
Wetheringsett, Stowmarket, Suffolk, IP14 5PW
Moseley Railway Museum
Apedale Country Park, Nr Newcastle-under-Lyme, Staffordshire, ST5 7LB
National Tramway Museum
Crich Tramway Village, Nr Matlock, Derbyshire, DE4 5DP
Nene Valley Railway
Wansford Station, Stibbington, Peterborough, PE8 6LR
Northamptonshire Ironstone Railway Trust
Hunsbury Hill Country Park, Hunsbury Hill Road, Northampton, NN4 9UW
Oswestry Bicycle & Railway Museum
Oswald Road, Oswestry, SY11 1RE
Rushden Historical Transport Museum
Station Approach, Rushden, Northants, NN10 0AW
Southwold Museum
9-11 Victoria Street, Southwold, Suffolk, IP18 6LD
Thinktank
Birmingham Science Museum, Millennium Point, Curzon Street,
  Birmingham, B4 7XG

Northern England

Beamish Open Air Museum
Beamish, Co Durham, DH9 0RG
Bradford Industrial Museum
Moorside Road, Bradford, West Yorkshire, BD2 3HP
Bury Transport Museum
Castlecroft Goods Warehouse, Castlecroft Road, Bury, Lancashire, BL9 0LN
Head of Steam – Darlington Railway Museum
North Road Station, Darlington, Co Durham, DL3 6ST
High Peak Junction Workshops
High Peak Junction, Whatstandwell, Matlock, Derbyshire, DE4 5HN
Isle of Man Railway Museum
Strand Road, Port Erin, Isle of Man
Leeds Industrial Museum
Armley Mills, Canal Road, Leeds LS12 2QF
Locomotion National Railway Museum
Soho Street, Shildon, Co Durham, DL4 1PQ
Manchester Museum of Science & Industry
Liverpool Road, Manchester, M3 4FP
Middleton Railway Trust
The Station, Moor Road, Hunslet, Leeds, LS10 2JQ
Monkwearmouth Station Museum
North Bridge Street, Sunderland, Tyne & Wear, SR5 1AP
Museum of Rail Travel
Ingrow West Railway Centre, Halifax Road, Ingrow, Keighley, West Yorkshire,
   BN22 8NJ
National Railway Museum
Leeman Road, York, YO2 4XJ
Norham Station Museum
Norham Station, Norham, Berwick-upon-Tweed, Northumberland TD15 2LW

North Tyneside Steam Railway & Stephenson Railway Museum
Middle Engine Lane, West Chirton, North Shields, Tyne & Wear, NE29 8DX
Ravenglass & Eskdale Railway Museum
Ravenglass Station, Ravenglass, Cumbria CA18 1SW
Threlkeld Quarry & Mining Museum
Threlkeld, Nr Keswick, Cumbria
Timothy Hackworth Victorian & Railway Museum
Soho Cottages, Hackworth Close, Shildon, Co Durham, DL4 2QX
Vintage Carriage Trust Railway Museum
Ingrow Station Yard, Halifax Road, Ingrow, Keighley, West Yorkshire BN22 8NJ
Wylam Railway Museum
Falcon Centre, Falcon Terrace, Wylam, Northumberland, NE41 8EE

Scotland

Alford Valley Railway Museum
Alford Station, Alford, Aberdeenshire, AB33 8HH
Glenfinnan Station Museum
Glenfinnan, Nr Fort William, Inverness-Shire, PH37 4LT
Riverside Museum
100 Pointhouse Place, Glasgow, G3 8RS
Scottish Industrial Railway Centre
Ayrshire Railway Preservation Group, Dunaskin Heritage Centre, Waterside,
   Ayrshire, KA6 7JS
Scottish Railway Exhibition
Bo'ness Station, Union Street, Bo'ness, West Lothian, EH51 9AQ

PUSH ME – PULL YOU/2
The story of the Lancashire & Yorkshire Railway's railmotors

U nlike the Great Western Railway's railmotors which had an integral
vertical boiler and driving cab, the Lancashire & Yorkshire Railway
under its Locomotive Superintendent George Hughes opted for a more novel
approach when designing its own railmotor.

However, prior to building his own railmotors, Hughes had bought two
such vehicles from the Taff Vale Railway (TVR) in 1905. They were built by
Kerr Stuart with bodies supplied by the Bristol Carriage & Wagon Works and
were used for several years on branch-line services around Bury and Bolton.
These test bed vehicles provided important lessons for Hughes and in 1906
he introduced the first of 18 railmotors which were built at Horwich Works.
At one end of the railmotor was a diminutive but conventional 0-4-0 tank
locomotive, fitted with outside cylinders and Walschaerts valve gear, which
was permanently attached to a single coach. The coach was supported at one
end by the locomotive and at the other end by a bogie. As with the GWR's
railmotors and auto trains a driving compartment at the far end of the trailer
coach allowed the driver to operate the train when the locomotive was pushing
from the rear. A cost-effective and successful design, the train was totally self-
contained and did not even need to be turned.

The two TVR railmotors were withdrawn in 1909 and by 1911 Horwich
had completed the production run of Hughes's own design. They could be seen

at work throughout Lancashire including the Bury to Holcombe Brook branch, the Southport to Altcar branch and along the Colne Valley. All of the L&YR's railmotors survived into LMS ownership with one (No. 10617) just scraping into the British Railway's era before it was withdrawn in 1948.

VITAL STATISTICS
Engine: 2 cylinders, 12in diameter x 16in stroke
Wheels: 3ft 7 ⅝in diameter on tread
Wheelbase (engine): 8ft; total wheelbase 54ft 8in
Boiler diameter: 4ft 3in
Heating surface (total): 509 sq ft
Grate area: 9.4 sq ft
Working pressure: 180lbs per sq in
Capacity of water tank: 550 gallons; capacity of coal bunker: 1 ton
Trailer car: Length over buffers: 69ft 5in; width of car body: 8ft 6¾in; length of car body: 47ft 6in; seating capacity: 56 passengers (all one class); luggage compartment: 340 cu ft
Total weight (loco and trailer): 47½ tons

L.Y.R. RAIL MOTOR COACH—(Views of Engine Front and Cab.)

A KENT RAILWAY VILLAGE
The story of Ashford Locomotive Works

The South Eastern Railway's main line from London to Dover via the small town of Ashford opened throughout in 1844. Soon, the expanding railway found its original railway works at New Cross too cramped so in 1846 the company set about finding a new, green fields site in Kent. Ashford was the chosen location because of its convenient location on the new main line. Buying 185 acres of land for £21,000, the SER built a new railway works along with 132 labourers' cottages around a village green, a pub, a Mechanics Institute, gas works, a school and public baths.

The first new mainline locomotive (a 'Hastings' Class 2-4-0 designed by Richard Cudworth) rolled out of the 26½-acre Locomotive Works in 1853. The adjoining Carriage & Wagon Works opened in 1855. The population of Ashford more than doubled between 1841 and 1861, by which time it had reached 7,000 and by 1882 the railway was employing around 1,300 workers. The main workshop was by far the biggest building, measuring 400ft long, 90ft wide and 28ft high. Adjacent to this the 640ft-long Carriage & Wagon Workshop included its own furnaces and a foundry. The SER merged with the London, Chatham & Dover Railway in 1899 after which Ashford became the main works for the newly formed South Eastern & Chatham Railway.

EXPRESS LOCOMOTIVE (4—4—0 TYPE), SOUTH EASTERN AND CHATHAM RAILWAYS.
Mr. H. S. Wainwright, M.Inst.C.E., *Locomotive Engineer*, Ashford.

After the 'Big Four Grouping' of 1923 Ashford became one of the three main workshops of the new Southern Railway, the others being at Brighton and Eastleigh. Construction of new coaches was transferred to Eastleigh and carriage repairs to Lancing in 1929. From that date Ashford concentrated mainly on locomotive and wagon construction and repair, both activities continuing into the BR era with the locomotive side ceasing in 1962 (when it was transferred to Eastleigh) and wagon repair and construction continuing until 1981. During World War II the works also built Browning machine guns for use on Blenheim fighter-bombers.

During its long history Ashford Locomotive Works built or rebuilt nearly 1,000 locomotives, the majority of them steam but, towards the end, diesel construction as well. New steam locomotives ranged from 239 designed by James Stirling for the SER, 196 designed by Harry Wainwright for the SE&CR and 118 designed by Richard Maunsell for the SE&CR and the Southern Railway. The latter included many famous classes that survived to see service on British Railways including 'N', 'N1' and 'U' Class 2-6-0s and 'W' Class 2-6-4 tanks. Under Southern Railway and later BR management the Works turned out 30 diesel shunters, 20 of Bulleid's 'Q1' Class 0-6-0s, 14 Stanier '8F' 2-8-0s, and the first two of the SR mainline diesel-electrics, Nos. 10201 and 10202 – the latter was the last locomotive to be built at Ashford when it was rolled out in the autumn of 1951.

SOUTHERN REGION
BRITISH RAILWAYS
ASHFORD LOCOMOTIVE WORKS
The main activity of the Locomotive Works at present is the repair of locomotives and manufacture of component parts

BRITISH RAILWAYS

GLASGOW TERMINI
The growth of railways in Glasgow

U ntil 1966 Glasgow proudly possessed four railway termini; today there are only two but more about this later. The first railway to enter Glasgow was the 4ft 6in gauge Garnkirk & Glasgow Railway, built primarily to carry coal, which opened in 1831. Initially using only two steam locomotives the railway also provided horsedrawn passenger coaches which terminated, inconveniently, at Townhead station on the outskirts of the city. Townhead remained the only station in Glasgow until 1841 when the Glasgow, Paisley & Greenock Railway and the Glasgow, Paisley, Kilmarnock & Ayr Railway opened their joint terminus at Bridge Street. Located just south of the Clyde near Glasgow Bridge it was conveniently positioned much closer to the city centre.

Queen Street station
Hot on the heels of Bridge Street station, Queen Street station was opened in 1842 by the Edinburgh & Glasgow Railway. The station had several bad features which still persist today – its cramped accommodation and short platforms made it a difficult station for long trains in steam-hauled days. On leaving the station drivers were faced with a dank and smoky tunnel under the Monkland Canal followed by the notorious 1 in 42 Cowlairs incline. Initially trains were hauled up the incline by a stationary steam engine operating a cable, a situation which persisted until 1909 when banking engines were introduced. An earlier experiment between 1844 and 1847 with two powerful banking locomotives had ceased because of damage to the track and tunnel. Banking of trains out of Queen Street continued until the final withdrawal of North British Type 2 diesels (Class 29 rebuilds) in 1971.

The Edinburgh & Glasgow Railway was absorbed by the North British Railway in 1865 with Queen Street becoming the latter company's Glasgow terminus. The station assumed another important role when it became the southern terminus of the West Highland Railway to Fort William on 11 August

1894 and by 1901 the opening of the Mallaig Extension brought even more traffic to the cramped station. In LNER and BR days the station was served by the 'Queen of Scots' Pullman train to and from King's Cross via Edinburgh Waverley, Harrogate and Leeds. Trains that normally terminated at Buchanan Street station were diverted to Queen Street when the former closed in 1966.

Buchanan Street station

As previously mentioned, Glasgow's first railway station was at Townhead but this was replaced by a more conveniently located terminus at Buchanan Street in 1849. Approached through a tunnel it was built by the Caledonian Railway as its main Glasgow terminus – however, the 'temporary' wooden structure wasn't replaced until 1933. Until the opening of Central station in

1879 CR trains from Carlisle and England terminated here. Once Central had opened, Buchanan Street lost its main purpose but continued to be used by CR and, later, LMS and BR trains to Oban via Callander (until 27 September 1965), to Inverness and to Aberdeen via Stirling, Perth and

Forfar. Notable among these were the three-hour Glasgow to Aberdeen expresses that saw Gresley's 'A4' Pacifics performing until their swansong in 1966. Buchanan Street was closed on 7 November 1966 and its remaining services were diverted to Queen Street.

St Enoch station

The opening of St Enoch station by the City of Glasgow Union Railway in 1876 heralded a third Anglo-Scottish trunk route with expresses travelling via the Midland Railway's Settle & Carlisle route and then via the Glasgow & South Western Railway via Dumfries. St Enoch was the first public building in Scotland to be lit by electricity and the neighbouring St Enoch Hotel which opened in 1879 echoed the grand Victorian Gothic style found at St Pancras,

400 miles to the south. Becoming part of the Glasgow & South Western
Railway in 1883, the station served destinations in Ayrshire and Dumfriesshire
as well as boat trains for Stranraer and Prince's Pier, Greenock. The main
express of the day was the 'Thames–Clyde' express which was introduced by
the LMS in 1927 but its timings via the Settle & Carlisle line were no match
for the rival West Coast Main Line – by 1962 the train took 2hr 20min longer
between St Pancras and St Enoch than the 'Royal Scot' did between Euston
and Central station. As with Buchanan Street, St Enoch became a victim of
Beeching's rationalisation policy and it closed on 27 June 1966 with trains
diverted to Central station. Sadly the 12-platform station and its twin glass and
iron train sheds along with the adjoining hotel were all demolished.

Central station

By the 1870s the Caledonian Railway's 'temporary' terminus at Buchanan
Street was already proving to be unsatisfactory for the growth of traffic. By
extending the existing line north of Bridge Street station and building a bridge

over the Clyde the CR could make a more direct approach into the city centre. Authorised in 1875, this short but important extension was opened to the new Central station in 1879. The bridge over the Clyde was built by William Arrol who later went on to build the second Tay Bridge and the Forth Bridge. The new cramped station soon proved to be too small and it was enlarged in 1890. However, within ten years, the station was again found to be unsatisfactory due to the increasing amount of traffic and it was rebuilt yet again, this time extending over Argyle Street with a glass-fronted bridge, building 13 platforms, an extra eight-track bridge over the Clyde and installing an electro-pneumatic power-operated signal box. The covered area of Argyle Street soon became famous as a gathering place for Highlanders visiting the city while the adjoining Central Hotel was a meeting place for the wealthy and famous. During the LMS era the station also witnessed the arrival and departure of several world-famous expresses including the 'Royal Scot', the streamlined 'Coronation Scot' (until 1939) and, in BR days, 'The Caledonian'. Diesel had

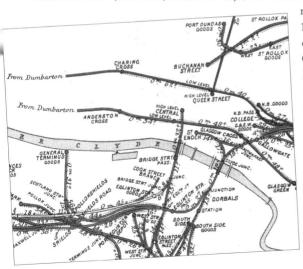

replaced steam by 1967 and by 1974 electrification of Glasgow suburban lines and the West Coast Main Line was complete. Today, Central station is the busiest station in the UK, outside of London, with passenger usage numbers reaching 29 million in 2010.

GOODBYE HAZEL, DORIS, AUDREY, VERA, GWEN and MONA
The story of the 'Brighton Belle'

Pullman cars were introduced by the London, Brighton & South Coast Railway in 1875. Six years later the company introduced the first all-Pullman train in the UK, the 'Pullman Limited' between London Victoria and Brighton. At the beginning of the 20th century the company changed the livery of all its coaches, including the Pullmans, to the now familiar brown umber and cream. This colour scheme was soon used on all Pullman coaches throughout the UK including the three new 35-ton 12-wheel vehicles introduced on the LBSCR service.

The LBSCR introduced a new Pullman train between Victoria and Brighton in 1908. Named the 'Southern Belle', this train made two returns each way on weekdays, taking exactly 60 minutes for the 50½-mile journey. It continued to operate as a steam-hauled service until 1933 when the London to Brighton line was electrified using third-rail pick-up. Three five-car all-Pullman electric multiple units then took over and the service was renamed the 'Brighton Belle' in 1934. In common with many other Pullman coaches the non-driving cars all received female names such as 'Hazel', 'Doris', 'Audrey', 'Vera', 'Gwen' and 'Mona'. The service was suspended during World War II but reinstated in 1946. By the early 1960s the train was operating three return journeys each weekday and two on Sundays but its age was beginning to show. Despite patronage by the great and the good the service was withdrawn by British Railways, amidst strong public protests, on 30 April 1972. Passengers travelling on the train on this last day were presented with a souvenir brochure and menu – the bar tariff makes interesting reading just one year after the introduction of decimalisation: ¼ bottle of champagne 75p; miniature Dubonnet 22p; miniature 'Royal Scot' whisky 37p; can of Guinness 15½p; can of Bulmer's Cider 12½p; small bottle ginger beer 8p. Those were the days!

Fortunately this wasn't the end for the 'Brighton Belle's' Pullman coaches as nearly all of them were saved – some of them ending up in pub gardens, two on the Keith & Dufftown Railway, while others were lovingly restored for use on the Venice Simplon Orient Express. Moves are now afoot to restore two of the driving cars and reunite them with their coaches so that the 'Brighton Belle' can run once again.

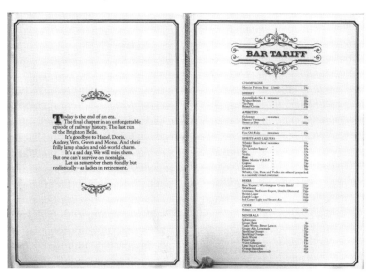

THE CLOCKWORK ORANGE
The story of the Glasgow Subway

Although not Glasgow's first underground railway (that distinction belongs to a 3-mile section of the Glasgow City & District Railway which opened in 1863), the Glasgow Subway is the third oldest underground metro system in the world.

With its ornate red sandstone headquarters at St Enoch, the Glasgow District Subway Corporation opened for business on 14 December 1896. It was unusual to say the least as it was built to a gauge of 4ft and trains on the 6½-mile double-track orbital railway were powered by a clutch and cable system. The two lines, burrowing under the River Clyde twice, were known as the Outer Circle and the Inner Circle and served 15 stations. Trains ran clockwise and anticlockwise respectively taking 24 minutes for a complete circuit but each line ran in a separate tunnel and the continuously moving cables were driven from a steam-powered winding station located south of the river near Shields Road station. Until modernisation in 1977 there was no direct connection with the railway's workshops at Govan so trains needing servicing had to be lifted off the running lines by a crane.

The original 'gripper' carriages that were used on the line were supplied by the Oldbury Railway Carriage & Wagon Company with 'non-gripper' trailer carriages supplied by Hurst Nelson of Motherwell. The subway was taken over by Glasgow Corporation in 1923 who went on to electrify the lines in 1935 and converted the original 'gripper' carriages to operate on 600V DC collected via a third rail. Another Subway oddity was that power for train lighting came from conductor rails located on the sides of the tunnels, a system that had been installed earlier when the line was still cable powered. Amazingly these late 19th – century vehicles, some retaining their original lattice gates, remained in service until 1977 when the whole system was closed down for modernisation. Many Glaswegians have fond memories of these old carriages as the backs of the seats were attached to the sides of the carriages while the seat itself was attached to an independently moving floor! Even members of the staff wore uniforms that had been introduced in 1901.

Modernisation of this by now antiquated transport system was well overdue when the subway was closed down in 1977. Three years later it was reopened with refurbished stations and new carriages supplied by Metro Cammell. Each train was made up of three carriages initially painted in a bright orange livery – hence the nickname 'The Clockwork Orange'. The depot at Broomloan was also refurbished and for the first time connected to the main system by rail. Nearly the entire contents of Merkland Street station were used to build a replica station in the Glasgow Museum of Transport (now closed but awaiting reopening in the new Riverside Museum).

Surprisingly the Glasgow Subway system has never been expanded although there are currently plans to add a new East Circle line with three interchange stations in time for the 2014 Commonwealth Games which are being held in the city. There are also other proposals for extending the Subway to the south and west, in places using existing disused railway tunnels.

The modern Subway Challenge: Is it possible to get off a clockwise Subway train at Buchanan Street station and get on the same train at St Enoch station? The train takes 55 seconds to travel between the two stations! Apparently someone has achieved this remarkable feat.

A RAILWAY COALITION
The story of the Cheshire Lines Committee

What became the second largest (by route miles after the Midland & Great Northern Joint Railway) and certainly the most profitable jointly owned railway in Britain, the Cheshire Lines Committee (CLC) was made up of five independent railways in the Manchester and Liverpool area. Its formation allowed its parent companies access to the lucrative trade from Liverpool Docks and the Manchester area, previously the domain of the London & North Western Railway and the Lancashire & Yorkshire Railway.

1. Backed by the Manchester, Sheffield & Lincolnshire Railway (successor to the Great Central Railway) and the Great Northern Railway, the 12¾-mile Cheshire Midland Railway opened throughout between Altrincham and Northwich in 1863.

2. The 2¾-mile Stockport & Woodley Junction Railway was also backed by the MS&LR and the GNR and opened in 1863.

3. The 8-mile Stockport, Timperley & Altrincham Junction Railway (backed by the MS&LR and the GNR) opened between Portwood and Deansgate (Altrincham) in 1865.

4. The 22¾-mile West Cheshire Railway from Northwich to Helsby opened completely in 1870 by which time it had become part of the CLC.

5. The 7-mile Chester & West Cheshire Junction Railway had already become part of the CLC when it opened between Mouldsworth Junction and Chester Northgate in 1875.

The CLC also worked trains on the independent 14-mile Southport &

Cheshire Lines Committee Extension Railway which opened between Aintree and Southport in 1884.

The Cheshire Lines Committee was officially formed as an independent concern on 15 August 1867 with equal shares held by the GNR, MSLR (later to become the Great Central Railway) and the Midland Railway. While the company owned its own rolling stock (including four Sentinel railcars from 1929) its locomotives were supplied by the owning companies, predominantly the Great Central until the Big Four Grouping of 1923 when that company became part of the LNER. The CLC remained independent until Nationalisation at the beginning of 1948. Several of its engine sheds, notably Heaton Mersey, Northwich and Trafford Park, remained in use until 1968, the last year of steam on BR.

During its lifetime the CLC was an extremely successful and profitable undertaking, running the most popular passenger service between its termini at Liverpool Central and Manchester Central and between Manchester and Chester. Opened in 1880, Manchester Central became one of the busiest stations in the UK. It closed in 1969 and is now an exhibition and conference centre while Liverpool Central, once the headquarters of the CLC, closed in 1972 and was demolished. The CLC routes between Manchester and Liverpool and between Manchester and Chester are still open to passengers today.

Freight traffic was even more important with the company serving the coalfields and industrial belt around Liverpool and Manchester, as well as Liverpool Docks and the salt mines and chemical works around Northwich.

CHINESE LAUNDRIES
The story of Bulleid's ill-fated 'Leader' Class

Oliver Bulleid, the Chief Mechanical Engineer of the Southern Railway from 1937 to 1947 and for the Southern Region of BR until 1950, was an innovative railway engineer best known for his air-smoothed Light Pacifics and 'Merchant Navy' Pacifics which did such sterling service on the Southern Region until the end of steam in 1967. Employing the most up-to-date technology, Bulleid was a world-leader in steam engine design but his final fling for the Southern Railway before departing for Ireland must surely rate as one of the most ill-conceived and poorly designed steam locomotive classes in the history of Britain's railways.

The 'Leader' Class started life in 1944 as a replacement for the ageing 'M7' 0-4-4 tank locos and was designed to incorporate many of the features found in Bulleid's utilitarian 'Q1' 0-6-0 locos. Following various drawing board proposals an 0-6-0+0-6-0 design was chosen. It featured two interchangeable six-wheeled steam driving bogies, an offset boiler placed inside a slab-sided bodywork not dissimilar to a modern diesel, duplicated driving cabs at each end linked by a corridor and a separate centrally located cab for the firebox and fireman. The driving bogies were each powered by three cylinders with the power transmitted to the driving wheels by an enclosed oil-bathed chain drive. Just to add to this nightmare scenario was the highly unusual sleeve valve arrangement which was hurriedly tested on an old LBSCR 'Atlantic' loco while 'Leader No.1' was being built.

An order for five 'Leader' Class locos was placed and work started on the prototype at Brighton Works in July 1947. Constant modifications to the design were made while work was hurriedly in progress and a start was also made on the other four members of the class. Nationalisation of Britain's railways in 1948 saw work continue on the prototype loco at Brighton and it emerged for trials, painted in grey with red and white lining, in June 1949. Sequentially following on from the 'Merchant Navy' numbering of 35XXX, the loco was numbered 36001. By then work had halted on the other four locos: No. 36002 was nearly complete; No. 36003 just needed its outer bodywork fitting; Nos. 36004 and 36005 had barely risen above their frames.

Untried and untested the slab-sided diesel-lookalike No. 36001 sallied forth around the south-eastern Division of the Southern Region, towing a dynamometer car and a train of empty carriages but immediately proved to be unreliable – the list of faults was endless and included heavy fuel and water consumption, badly fitted cylinder rings, poor braking, collapsed firebox linings and uneven balance. The crew worked in confined spaces in appallingly hot conditions leading to the locomotive being nicknamed the 'Chinese Laundry'! While some of these problems were addressed it was all to no avail despite Oliver Bulleid postponing his departure to Ireland in order to oversee the trials. The loco made its last run, reportedly with some success, on 2 November 1950, but having already spent large amounts of taxpayers' money on the unreliable locomotive British Railways was having none of it and the project was cancelled in 1951.

Not surprisingly neither No. 36001 nor the four other unfinished locos survived and they were quietly broken up for scrap. Bulleid went on to become CME of Irish Railways (CIE) where he designed his famous turf-burning locomotive.

A RAILWAY-OWNED ELECTRIC TRAMWAY
The story of the Grimsby & Immingham Tramway

Originally conceived by the Manchester, Sheffield & Lincolnshire Railway, the forerunner of the Great Central Railway, the massive new docks at Immingham at the mouth of the River Humber in north Lincolnshire were officially opened by King George V in 1912. With his eye on the European market, the GCR's forward-looking director Sam Fay was knighted by the king at the same time.

Equipped with state-of-the-art coal-handling facilities the docks covered an area of 45 acres and had its own internal railway system. The workforce for the construction of the docks and later to run them was mainly drawn from the neighbouring port of Grimsby and a key factor to the smooth running of the operation was the building of an electric tramway linking the two locations. This replaced a steam railcar service on the earlier Grimsby District Light Railway which had been built by the dock contractor.

Opened in 1912 by the Great Central Railway, the electric tramway ran for five miles, mainly on a straight route across marshland but partly through the

streets of Immingham and Grimsby, from Immingham Town to Corporation Bridge at Grimsby. A short branch also led to Immingham Dock Eastern Jetty. The depot for the line was at Pyewipe north of Grimsby and passing places were provided on the single track main line across the marshes.

Operating on a 500V DC current, the trams collected current from an overhead line held up by wooden poles. Initially services were provided by a fleet of 12 54ft-long single-decker bogie trams and four shorter versions for working in the streets of Grimsby.

The tramway became part of the LNER in 1923 and then the nationalised British Railways in 1948 when the trams were repainted in a green livery. To cope with increased demand after World War II when new industries were being built along the Humber a large fleet of redundant secondhand trams was purchased from the Gateshead & District Tramways Company in 1951. With business booming in the 1950s the tramway continued to operate until 1961 when the building of new roads and the introduction of buses finally brought about its closure. Even the *Ian Allan ABC locospotters' guide* of Summer 1961 lists 26 Grimsby & Immingham electric trams on the stockbooks at this late stage. Fortunately one of the original Great Central tramcars has been preserved as part of the National Collection and two of the former Gateshead tramcars, Nos. 20 and 26, have been preserved and can be seen at Crich Tramway Museum and Beamish Open Air Museum respectively.

INDEX

1400 Class 81

`A2/3' Class 90
`A4' Class 89–90
Aberdeen to Glasgow
    19–20
artists, railway 48–50
Ashford Works 124–5
autotrains 80–1

`B1' Class 90–1
Banbury to Oxford
    20
Bath Green Park 98
`Battle of Britain'
    Class 88
Beeching cuts 81, 128
Blackfriars 92
`Bournemouth Belle'
    104–5
`Brighton Belle'
    130–1
`Bristolian, The' 63–4
British Railways 8–9,
    26–7, 31, 36, 48–9,
    53, 58, 62, 82–3, 87,
    108–10, 113, 123,
    125, 127, 129, 131,
    135–9
Broad Street 92
Brunel, I. K. 72, 96
Buchanan Street
    19–20, 127, 133
Bulleid, Oliver 136–7

buses, railway-owned
    23–5

Caledonian 14–15, 62,
    108, 127–9
Cambrian Coach
    Express 64–5
Campbeltown &
    Machrihanish 55
Cannon Street 92
Carlisle to Glasgow
    18–19
`Castle' Class 63–5, 88
Central station 18–19,
    128–9
Channel Tunnel 46
Charing Cross 92–3
Charlton Viaduct 99
`Cheltenham Flyer'
    59
Cheshire Lines Com.
    134–5
Christmas traffic
    10–12
Churchward `Saint'
    33–4
`Clan' Class 6MT 36
Class `8K' 62
    2-8-0 62
`Coronation' Class 36
Cowlairs 108–9
Craven Arms 17
crime 43–5
Cuneo, Terence 49–50

cut-backs 13

`Devon Belle' 105–6

East & West Junction
    56–7
Edinburgh Haymarket
    111
Egyptian National
    26–7
Elan Valley 66–8
Euston 93
Evesham, Redditch &
    Stratford-upon-
    Avon 56
express trains 16, 107

Fay, Sam 29, 138
Fenchurch Street 93
`Flying Scotsman'
    59, 77
Fowler `Patriot'
    Class 35

Gartell Light 99
`Geoffrey Chaucer'
    18–19
ghost stations 37–9
Glasgow Subway
    132–3
Gloucester Eastgate
    6–8
Gloucester to
    Hereford 111

Gloucestershire
    Regiment 8–9
`Grange' Class 34–5
Great Central 57, 62,
    79, 95, 135, 138–9
Great Eastern 25, 62,
    78, 94
Great North of
    Scotland 25
Great Northern 17,
    48, 134–5
Great Western 9, 11–
    12, 23–5, 28–30,
    33–5, 42–3, 52–3,
    61–5, 69, 72–6,
    80–1, 87–8, 96–7,
    100, 103, 107
Grimsby &
    Immingham 138–9

`Hall' Class 112
Hassall, John 48
Hawksworth
    `County' 33
Highland 109–10,
    114–15
Holborn Viaduct 93
House of Commons
    46–7

Inverurie 109

Kilmarnock 110
`King' Class 63

King's Cross 93–4
King's Lynn to
    Norwich 112

Lancashire &
    Yorkshire 122–3,
    134
`Leader' Class 136–7
Light Railway
    Transport League
    70–1
lineside passes 41
Liverpool &
    Manchester 42
Liverpool Street 94
Lochgorm 109–10
London &
    Birmingham 28, 42
London Bridge 94–5
London, Brighton &
    South Coast 95,
    97, 130
London, Chatham &
    Dover 92–3, 95,
    97, 124
London & Croydon
    94–5
London & Greenwich
    94–5
London, Midland &
    Scottish 7, 21–2,
    26, 35–6, 48–9, 58,
    62, 77, 89, 100, 103,
    107, 110, 128–9
London & North
    Eastern 21, 25–7,
    32–3, 59, 62, 77,
    89–91, 100, 103,
    105–6, 109, 127,

135, 138
London & North
    Western 10, 12, 16,
    25, 43, 48, 56, 61,
    82, 134
London & South
    Western 10, 12,
    28–30, 61, 97, 104
London Waterloo 39
Lynton & Barnstaple
    23–4

Marylebone 95
Midland 6, 10, 28–9,
    51–2, 56–7, 61, 82,
    96, 135
Midland & South
    Western Junction
    28–31
Midsomer Norton
    98–9
museums, railway
    116–21

Nidd Valley Light
    68–9
North British 14–15,
    62, 108
North Eastern 43, 62,
    68–9
Northampton &
    Banbury Junction
    56–7
nuclear power stations
    84–6

Paddington 96
Parliamentary trains
    39

`Patriot' Class 35, 89
Peppercorn `A1' Class
    32, 90
Pines Express 82–3
police, railway 42–5
Pullmans 104–5, 127,
    130–1

Queen Street station
    126–7

railmotors 34, 122–3
Royal Engineers,
    Railway Operating
    Division 60–2,
    79
`Royal Scot' 22, 77,
    129

St Enoch 127–8, 133
St Pancras 96–7
St Rollox 108
Sentinel Steam
    Railcars 26–7
Severn Railway
    Bridge 51–3
shed bashing 40–1
Sheringham 111
Shillingstone 99
Snailbeach District
    54, 61
Solway Viaduct 14–15
Somerset & Dorset
    Joint 26, 77, 82,
    98–9
South Eastern 44–5,
    92, 94–5, 124
Southern 26–7, 79,
    88, 95, 100, 104–6,

125, 136
`Southern Belle' 59,
    104, 130
Stratford-upon-Avon
    & Midland
    Junction 56–8

telegraph 43
Townhead 126, 127
train names 78–9,
    87–91
tram lines 70–1,
    138–9
`Two Tunnels
    Greenway' 98

wagon shortages 47
war 8–9, 60–2, 79, 82,
    100–3
War Department
    Light 61
water works railways
    66–9
Waterloo 97
Wilkinson, Norman
    48–9
Woodham's scrapyard
    32–5
works 41, 107–10,
    124–5

MORE AMAZING TITLES

LOVED THIS BOOK?

Tell us what you think and you could win another fantastic book
from David & Charles in our monthly prize draw.

www.lovethisbook.co.uk

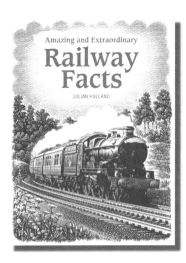

**AMAZING & EXTRAORDINARY
RAILWAY FACTS**
JULIAN HOLLAND
ISBN: 978-0-7153-2582-7

MORE AMAZING & EXTRAORDINARY RAILWAY FACTS
JULIAN HOLLAND
ISBN: 978-0-7153-3622-9

AMAZING & EXTRAORDINARY FACTS: GREAT BRITAIN
STEPHEN HALLIDAY
ISBN: 978-0-7153-3907-7

PICTURE CREDITS

Photographs used in this book have come from many sources. Some have been supplied by the photographers and picture libraries below. Others have been bought on the open market, sometimes with no information about the original photographer. Wherever possible, photographers or collections have been acknowledged, but some images inevitably remain anonymous, despite attempts at tracing or identifying them. If photographs have been used without due credit or acknowledgement where credit is due, through no fault of our own, apologies are offered.

All photographs and illustrations are from the author's collection apart from the following:

Ben Ashworth: 7, 30
Hugh Ballantyne: 58, 63
Henry Casserley: 29, 31, 35, 57, 60, 62, 133, 135, 137, 139
John Goss: 87, 130
Tony Harden: 11, 23, 55, 69, 128
Michael Mensing: 94
Colour-Rail: 104
Milepost 92 ½: 106
Science & Society Picture Library via Getty Images: 50
Soldiers of Gloucestershire Museum: 9